Way to Grow

Way to Grow

Over 100 hacks for green-fingered greatness

Simon Akeroyd

Contents

Introduction 6

Grow
8

Cardboard seed pots	10
Mix small seeds with sand	12
Sow seeds standing up	13
Sow large seeds on their side	14
Seed tray from a pallet	15
Collect seeds for free	16
Store seeds in cheese boxes	18
DIY seed envelopes	20
Milk carton propagator	22
Milk carton cloche	23
Toilet roll planters	24
Free plant labels	26
Use a pot to make a planting hole	30
Plant sunflowers facing east	31
Storage box mini greenhouse	32
Take a lavender cutting	34
Sweet pea tip cuttings	35
Propagate rosemary	36
Take hardwood rose cuttings	38
Vertical strawberry planter	40
Grow early peas in gutters	41
White pebbles for ripening fruit	42
Grow a cactus from dragon fruit	44
Grow carrots for flowers	46
Hose and rake seed driller	48
Make a trug from sticks	50
Tool unit from a pallet	51
Mesh potato tower	52
Fork handle dibber	54
Rake head storage	55
Store hand tools in sand	56

Protect
58

Slugs and snails	60
Ladybird hotel against aphids	64
Sticky tape against blackfly	65
Feather and potato bird scarer	66
Milk against mildew	70
Rotate your veg crops	71
Spice jar eye protectors	72
Decoy strawberries	74
Spicy bird seed	75
Flowerpot earwig catchers	76
Container bulb saver	78
Catmint to divert cats	80
Companion planting	81
De-weed your patio	82

Nurture
84

Free liquid plant food	86
Two-bucket wormery	90
Make leaf mould	92
Mole hill magic	94
Potassium power	95
Space-saving composting	96
Compost bin rat repeller	98
Chop your compost	99
Recycled pallet compost bay	100
Colour your compost	102
Rotate your compost	103
Banana skin plant food	104
Coffee booster	106
Eggshell fertilizer	107
Bindweed liquid feed	108

Maintain
110

Mulch your borders	112
Perfect your lawn edges	113
No dig	114
Coat hanger hoe	118
Collect rainwater	120
Wildlife-friendly watering can	122
Hands-free watering	124
Cotton bud irrigation system	126
Milk bottle watering can	128
Recycled bag watering	130
Grow dandelions	131
Aerate your lawn	132
Spoon water diffuser	134
Chelsea chop	136
Secateur savvy	138
Deadhead for more flowers	140
No-fuss rose pruning	142
Anti-sting sock gauntlets	143
Grow tomatoes up strings	144
Recycle your tights	146
Use a clove hitch	150
Handy string saver	152
Terracotta pot watering	154
Pea sticks from prunings	156

Design
158

Use a colour wheel	160
Shape your lawn	162
Wheelbarrow chair	163
Make a dead hedge	164
Three sisters	166
Plant a pumpkin right way round	167
Toilet roll bird feeder	168
Parasol grapevine trainer	170
Simple pallet raised bed	171
Hosepipe raised bed	172
Shoe rack herb garden	174
Croc containers	176
Mini terrarium	178
Quick stick seat	180
Keyhole gardening	182
Edimental plants	184

Index	188
Acknowledgements	191
About the author	192

Introduction

This book is about the magic of gardening, and thinking outside the box "hedge" and what we are traditionally taught. Whether you are a beginner gardener, or a bit of a green-fingered pro, I hope it inspires you to come up with your own creative ways to create a little bit of plant paradise for yourself.

You will discover gardening tips I learned from professional and amateur gardeners I've met during my gardening career. Other hacks came from me experimenting in my own garden in Devon and learning by trial and error, or should I say trowel and error (ahem).

I've been incredibly lucky to have spent the last 30 years doing two things that I'm passionate about: gardening and writing about gardening. I've had the opportunity to work in some of the most spectacular gardens on the planet. I've learned so many handy gardening hacks along the way, which are impossible to learn from a book. Until now, of course!

Gardening can sometimes feel a bit baffling – and way too technical. My first degree was in philosophy, and one of the many things I discovered is that there is an infinite number of ways to do anything. It's just your way ... and once you start gardening, you will discover what works for you.

Plants want to grow, and we just need to find simple ways to encourage them. For that reason, I'm hoping this book will help demystify some of the horticultural terminology, and give you great tips to help you grow plants and create a lovely garden.

As you turn the pages of this book, I hope you are inspired to give these hacks a try. It's not intended as a manual to tell you what you should or shouldn't be doing in the garden. These are my suggestions, and tips that work for me. Please do try them, but also find your own way. That's how you become an accomplished gardener.

Enjoy experimenting with different ways of growing, pruning, cultivating, and caring for your plants. Learn to love getting your hands dirty, pulling on your gardening boots, and observing the scents, sounds, and visual delights that walking among plants can give you. Then you'll truly find your own piece of horticultural heaven.

Hack 1
Cardboard seed pots

We seem to end up with loads of surplus cardboard these days, due to online shopping and retailers using more sustainable packaging than plastic. One of my favourite things to do with it is to make plant pots to sow my seeds into.

These pots are very easy to make using a few items you already have at home, such as recycled cardboard. You can cut your cardboard to the desired height with scissors before or after it goes in the bucket of water. Once you have shaped it nicely, leave the cardboard to dry in the sun for a few hours (or in a warm place indoors), still wrapped around the glass, to firm up the shape. You should be left with a lovely shaped plant pot, which you can fill §with compost and sow a seed into.

You can also make plant pots from newspaper folded into thirds. Roll around a jar in the same way as opposite, with 5cm (2in) newspaper overhanging the open end. Tuck in the overhang, then remove the jar and press down firmly to create a base.

Plant the pot too

Once the seed has germinated you can plant the pot (cardboard or newspaper) directly into the soil. The bottom will quickly decompose, enabling the roots to stretch out into the soil below it. This is great, as it avoids disturbing the seedling's roots when planting out.

how to roll your own pots

01 Immerse a piece of waste cardboard in a bucket of water and leave for a few minutes to become completely wet.

02 Take it out of the bucket and place a glass jar on top, leaving surplus cardboard at one end of the jar. Roll the wet cardboard round the jar.

03 Squash the excess cardboard around the bottom of the jar to create the base of the pot. Once the cardboard has dried, remove the jar.

04 Fill your plant pot with compost and sow a seed in it. The whole thing can be planted out when the seedling is ready (see box).

Hack 2
Mix small seeds with sand

Some vegetable seeds, such as parsnip and carrot, are tiny. If you have slightly chubby fingers like me, this makes them very difficult to use. This tip makes it much easier.

Grab an empty spice jar and half fill it with sand (your carrier). I've used ash from my log burner as a carrier too, although don't do this too often, as ash can increase the pH in your soil (see p.95). Tip your tiny seeds into the jar, secure the lid, and give it a good shake so that the seeds get thoroughly mixed into the sand.

Create a seed drill (see p.48) and shake the contents of the jar along it, distributing the sand and seed as equally as possible. Brush the soil back over the sand and seed, and mark both ends of the row with a cane so you don't forget where you sowed them. I place the spice jar over the sharp end of the cane, so I don't accidentally damage an eye when working in the garden (see also p.72).

Leaf trick

Once seeds have started growing and you need to prick them out, hold each seedling by a leaf and not the stem. That's because if the stem breaks you've lost the plant, but if a leaf breaks, the seedling should recover.

Hack 3
Sow seeds standing up

If you suffer from a bad back, some gardening jobs might be uncomfortable or even impossible for you. One job in particular can require lots of bending down and backache: seed sowing directly into the ground. This hack can help.

You can of course grow plants in raised beds, which saves having to constantly bend down to the ground. If you don't have those, you could try sowing seeds with a hollow length of piping, tube, or stick.

Use a long-handled hoe or the edge of a rake to draw out a drill, or a long stick as a dibber to create a hole for sowing seeds into. Take a long pipe or hollow stick and hold one end above the hole. Roll the seed down the pipe from the top and into the hole or drill. Then use your foot to brush the soil back over the seed. You will find this saves you lots of unnecessary backache as there is no need for bending down.

Back savers

Where possible, use long-handled tools (as well as your sowing pipe) in the garden, and bend your knees when lifting to protect your back. Rather than bending over like a hinge, try squatting or sitting on a kneeling pad or stool.

Hack 4
Sow large seeds on their side

Large seeds such as courgette, pumpkin, and melon can rot if you sow them flat in the compost. Avoid disappointment with this easy hack.

When you water big seeds, the water tends to puddle or collect on the large surface and doesn't drain away, which can result in the seed not germinating and instead rotting in the damp conditions. For this reason, it's a good idea to always sow large seeds on the edge as shown, as the water will easily run off down the sides, preventing them rotting away.

Hack 5
Seed tray from a pallet

I've got a seed tray in my potting shed that I made over 20 years ago from recycled timber, and I'm hoping it will last at least as long again. I have since made lots more. They look so much nicer than plastic ones, and it's better for the environment.

This project is fairly easy, requiring few DIY skills. After all, even I can make them! Another aspect I like about wooden seed trays is that the compost doesn't seem to dry out as quickly. Maybe the timber holds some of the moisture. Check the pallets are heat-pressure treated (see box, page 51).

Remove 6 slats from the pallet. I tend to saw them at the required length rather than try to crowbar them off, as it's easier. You will need 2 x 35cm (14in) for the long sides, 2 x 20cm (8in) for the short sides, and 2 x 35cm (14in) for the base.

Nail or screw the two lengths and two widths of the seed tray together to form a rectangle, like the sides of a box with no base. Then attach the two lengths to make the base of the seed tray, leaving a gap between the slats for drainage. That's it - you could stencil your name on the side for a vintage look.

Finally, fill with seed compost and sow your seeds. Don't forget to label your plants!

You will need

+ Old wooden pallet
+ Saw
+ Tape measure
+ Hammer and nails

Hack 6
Collect seeds for free

If you see a plant you fancy in a friend's garden, don't be afraid to ask if you can have some seed. And you can collect seed from a plant you grew yourself and particularly enjoyed. Either way, waiting until the end of the season and collecting the seed can save you cash.

It's important to wait until the seed is fully ripe, or it won't germinate. In the case of vegetables, you will need to leave a few unharvested so that they can go on to form seeds. Harvest on a dry day. I like to cut the entire seed head off a plant and turn it upside down into a paper bag. Once you've got your seeds home, ensure they are fully dry before placing them into envelopes, labelling them, and storing them somewhere dry for the following season.

Not all plants will come true from seed, so there can be some variation between the original plant and the offspring that their seeds produce. However, this is how we create even better varieties, and although there may be a few disappointments along the way, it is a great way to discover something new.

Some plants require a process of chilling (stratification) before they will germinate. (If you're unsure, a quick internet search will tell you if it is required.) Place your seeds in a plastic bag with a handful of compost and leave it to chill in a fridge for a few weeks. Then remove the bag, tip the seeds into an envelope, and store until you're ready to sow.

Hack 7
Store seeds in cheese boxes

I don't need any more excuses to buy cheese, but if I did, then this would be a good one. Did you know that the round wooden boxes that are often used to contain Camembert, Brie, and other soft cheeses make excellent storage boxes for your seeds?

Simply remove the cheese – don't forget to eat it – and tip your seeds into the box. The great thing about these boxes is that they are easily stackable. They are nice and light, and keep the seed dry and dark – the perfect environment for seed storage. And if you've tipped out too many when sowing, it's much more convenient to tip your seeds back into a big box than trying to get them into a small paper seed packet or envelope with one hand.

Easy labelling

I use masking tape and an indelible pen to label my boxes. Stick a strip of tape around the boxes to make them easy to identify at a glance. The following year, it is easy to peel off and replace.

Hack 8
DIY seed envelopes

This is how I make my own seed envelopes. I collect masses of seeds from my garden so I find this hack really useful.

Seeds are best stored in envelopes as they are dry and dark, and it's a cheap option. I have hundreds of envelopes that I collect seeds in each autumn, but there is no need to buy them. They are so quick and easy to make from just a sheet of paper.

how to make a handy envelope

01 Fold the corner of a sheet of paper over to create a square. Cut along the fold to create a triangle. Have the long edge in front of you.

02 Fold the point of the right-hand corner across to meet the left-hand side, keeping the top of the fold parallel with the long bottom edge.

03 Repeat with the left-hand corner. Fold the top flap that is nearest you down to create an envelope.

04 Label it before filling the envelope with seed, or it will be too bumpy to write on.

05 Fill your envelope with seed, then bring the final flap down at the top to seal it.

06 I find folding the flap over is enough to secure the envelope, but you can use sticky tape if it doesn't stay shut.

Hack 9
Milk carton propagator

Instead of throwing away plastic milk cartons you can use them to make useful mini propagation units. These will provide extra warmth for your seedlings and enable you to start growing plants earlier in the year.

Use the sharp end of the scissors to create a few holes in the bottom of the milk carton. These holes will provide drainage and prevent the compost from getting too damp, causing seedlings to rot.

Using scissors, carefully cut around your milk carton halfway up, leaving one side uncut. This uncut side will form a hinge, so that you can open and close the propagator.

Now you can fill your new propagator with compost and sow your seeds. To provide extra warmth, simply pull down the top half of the milk carton. If it doesn't stay down, use sticky tape to hold it in place. If you want to prevent too much humidity building up, you can open the lid.

I often use plastic supermarket muffin boxes as makeshift mini propagators, too, as they usually have a lid. Use a skewer to poke drainage holes in the bottom if necessary. Water the compost regularly as it can dry out quite quickly if it's warm, and lift the lid to cool your seedlings on really hot days.

You will need

+ Scissors
+ Clean two-litre milk carton
+ Compost
+ Packets of seeds

Hack 10
Milk carton cloche

If you want to get plants off to an early start in the season, or provide some extra protection towards the end of the season, you can protect them from the cold by using cloches.

The simplest and cheapest cloche for your garden is made from a plastic milk container. Just use scissors to remove the base and place the top section over a vulnerable plant if frosts are predicted. It will also provide extra warmth early or late in the season. Remove the cap on warmer days to increase air circulation and reduce humidity.

You can of course buy cloches. Traditional ones are bell-shaped and made of glass (cloche is French for bell), and you can buy cheaper plastic versions to protect individual plants. If you have rows of plants to protect you can buy tunnel cloches, which are a bit like mini polytunnels.

Hack 11
Toilet roll planters

Instead of sowing seeds into plastic pots, you can use cardboard toilet roll tubes. So don't throw them away, but save them up until you need to do some seed sowing.

The important thing here is to create a solid bottom for the toilet roll tubes to stop the soil falling out. Make as many as you need, then add some compost and sow a seed in each.

Once the seed has germinated you can plant it directly in the soil, complete with the cardboard tube. The bottom of the pot will quickly decompose, enabling the roots to stretch out into the soil, and the plant to grow.

how to plant your loo roll

01 Take your cardboard tube and make four 5cm (2in) slits, equally spaced around the bottom of the tube, to create flaps.

02 Fold all four flaps into the centre and press firmly to create a base for your planter. Now you can add soil and plant a seed.

Bury your pot

Make sure all the cardboard is buried when you plant your seedling. If any cardboard is left uncovered, it can wick moisture out of the soil, leaving it dry.

Hacks 12–17
Free plant labels

You can make beautiful free plant labels at home from natural materials found in the garden or in surrounding countryside. It's so easy to do, requiring next to no DIY skills (even I can do it), and they look so much nicer than the plastic labels for sale.

A common mistake gardeners make is forgetting to label our plants. Or we just think we'll remember what we sowed. By a few weeks later, though, we've completely forgotten and have no idea what our emerging seedlings are.

Plastic or wooden labels are available to buy. However, I much prefer to make my own. Partly because it's free, but also because they look much nicer than bought plastic ones, and finally, because I like to recycle material.

Pen or pencil?

In some cases I'll use an indelible pen so that it doesn't run when it rains or if I splash them when watering. I generally use this when a pencil won't stand out clearly enough. However, for most of my seedlings I use a pencil to label the plants, written onto wooden cutlery or small plastic labels that I've recycled from milk cartons. The advantage of using pencil is that you can recycle labels again and again by rubbing the writing off and rewriting the new name.

Plastic milk cartons

Save your milk cartons as they make brilliant plant labels that are completely free and reusable, especially if you write with a pencil (see p.26). After rinsing your carton, simply cut it up into strips about 10cm (4in) long and 1cm (½in) wide. You can of course do the same with margarine tubs and yogurt pots.

Stones

I often pick up largish stones or pebbles and use an indelible pen to write the name of the plants that I've sown or planted. I like to use these at the base of fruit trees I grow in pots and place the pebble on the surface of the compost.

Sticks

I like to recycle sticks left over from pruning my fruit trees. Look for sticks that are about 20cm (8in) long and 1–2cm (½–¾in) in diameter. Use a knife or the blade of your secateurs to carefully slice off a 5cm- (2in-) long slither of bark at the top end of the stick to create a flat surface. Then use an indelible pen to write the name of the plant. You can also cut or whittle the bottom end – or use a pencil sharpener if the stick is the right diameter – to make a sharp point for pushing into the soil easily. Another advantage of using sticks is that you can erase the name of a previous plant by scraping off the writing with a knife.

Wine corks

No need to sling your corks into the bin after you're opened a bottle of your favourite tipple. Instead, write the name of your plant onto the cork with an indelible pen, then push onto one of those wooden stirrers you get for takeaway coffee. A bamboo skewer for making kebabs works well, too. Insert the other end into the pot to give you an attractive, bespoke plant label.

Wooden pegs and disposable cutlery

I love the look of wooden plant labels and if you have a spare wooden clothes peg, you can write the name of your plant straight onto one side and clip it to the edge of a pot. You can also use disposable wooden cutlery or lollipop sticks. Simply rinse after using and dry off, before writing on them and inserting next to your plant to remind yourself what you sowed.

Hack 18
Use a pot to make a planting hole

When planting up your containers, it can be difficult to work out the size of the hole needed for each plant. This is a really simple hack to give you the perfect size.

Half-fill your container with compost, ensuring that you have covered the drainage holes at the bottom with stones or broken crocks. This prevents the compost from leaching out when you water your plants.

Place your new plant, in its pot, on the surface of the compost. Make sure the top of the plant pot sits just below the top of the container. If it doesn't, then you might want to adjust the amount of compost below the pot. Once you are happy with the level you can then pack the compost in around the plant pot until it reaches just below the top of the container.

Remove the plant pot from the hole. It will have left you with an indentation in the compost which is the perfect size for your plant to slot into. All you need to do now is remove the plant from its pot and place it in the newly created hole. Don't forget to water your plant to help it settle in.

Hack 19
Plant sunflowers facing east

Sunflowers are incredibly clever. Originating from the hot plains of Central America, they are real sun worshippers.

The flowerheads face the sun and move with it as it crosses the sky. At night the flowerheads turn back so that they are facing the rising sun first thing in the morning. However, once they have reached their desired height, they stop tracking the sun and remain facing east. So if you are planting sunflowers, make sure that you plant them on the east side of your garden, to ensure they will face you. If you plant them on the west, you may well find that it is your neighbours who are enjoying their gorgeous yellow faces, while you end up looking at the backs of the sunflowers' heads for the remainder of summer.

Follow the sun

Sunflowers track the sun during the day, a phenomenon known as heliotropism (moving towards the light).

Hack 20
Storage box mini greenhouse

You can easily run out of warm, frost-free growing space to germinate all your emerging seedlings in spring. Not all of us can afford a greenhouse and cold frames, or have the space for them. Here is an economical solution.

If there's no more space on your kitchen windowsill and it is too cold to grow seedlings outside, don't despair. An easy hack is at hand – plastic storage boxes, which you may already have at home.

Place the lid of your storage box in a sunny, sheltered spot in the garden. Then arrange your plants on the lid. Put the box on top of the lid but prop up one edge on a brick to allow air to circulate. You can sit the brick on its side or, on warmer days, on its end to raise the storage box higher and increase the flow of air. You can remove the box completely on really hot days. Just remember to replace the box and close firmly in the evening if cold weather or overnight frosts are predicted. It is worth putting another brick or heavy object on top of the box to weigh it down and ensure it doesn't blow away in high winds.

Adjustable air circulation

I turn my box upside-down like this as it allows for better air circulation through the plants. This reduces the risk of humidity building up around the plants, which can lead to fungus such as mildew.

Hack 21
Take a lavender cutting

This aromatic herb is a gorgeous plant to have in your garden. They are lovely evergreen structures for edging a border, and bees and other pollinators adore the purple flowers. If you don't already have one, no problem, because it is very easy to take a cutting from a friend's lavender plant.

I find the best type of cutting to take for propagating lavender is a semi-ripe one. This means that the lower part of the stem is starting to turn woody, but the top part is still soft from the growth it made earlier in the year. The best time to do this is between mid- and late summer.

Look for a healthy new stem that is about 15cm (6in) long, ideally non-flowering. Cut it with secateurs and then trim the cutting at the base just below a bud. Insert half the length of the cutting into a gritty compost mix. This is because lavender, like many Mediterranean herbs, requires a free-draining soil. They will quickly rot in heavy soil with poor drainage. I leave my cuttings outside over summer, watering them once a week if it's dry. By the following spring your cuttings should be ready to plant where you want them in the garden.

Hack 22
Sweet pea tip cuttings

One of the lovely aspects of gardening is that it can often feel like the gift that keeps giving. Making extra sweet pea plants at no cost is a classic example. If you want to double the number of sweet peas you have to plant in the garden, here is what you need to do.

When the sweet pea plants reach about 20cm (8in) high, cut back the new shoots by half to just above a pair of leaves. Don't worry about harming the current plants. Gardeners often pinch out the new growth at this stage anyway as it means you'll get bushier plants and more flowers.

Put the sweet pea cutting in a jar with 2cm (¾in) water. Place on a sunny windowsill and keep topping up the water to 2cm (¾in). Soon you will notice roots forming in the water, and hopefully new growth at the top. These sweet pea cuttings can be planted into compost and grown on in the same way as new seedlings. If you get sweet peas growing early in the season (they can be grown from as early as autumn), you can continue to take cuttings from the former cutting until late spring, giving you an almost endless supply of sweet peas.

Hack 23
Propagate rosemary

Rosemary is one of my favourite herbs to grow. Not only does it have a gorgeous aromatic flavour, but it is a great structural plant in the garden and I love the deep blue flowers that can appear on the darkest of winter days.

Instead of buying an expensive rosemary bush, buy a packet from the supermarket and use one of the sprigs as a cutting. The rosemary should produce a few roots after several weeks in water, which you can top up as necessary. You can move a single cutting into gritty compost in a 9cm (3½in) pot to enable it to continue growing, or group several cuttings into a larger pot as shown.

Once the cuttings have established a good root system and show signs of healthy growth from the top, they can be planted out into the garden, after the risk of frosts is over. Alternatively, plant your rosemary in a larger pot and keep it on a patio or by the back door so that it is easy for you to pop out and harvest a few sprigs.

Cutting edge trick

Put a few cuttings in one pot to save space. One tip is to insert the cuttings around the edge of the pot, rather than in the centre. This is because the compost dries quicker at the side of the pot after watering, meaning there is less chance of them rotting. It is also said that when roots hit the side of the pot they are forced to branch out, and therefore spread, which develops a better root system.

how to grow rosemary plants

01 Select a straight, non-flowering, healthy stem of rosemary about 15cm (6in) long.

02 Using scissors, cut just below a bud at the base, as this will stimulate roots to grow.

03 Stick the base of your rosemary cuttings in about 5cm (2in) water and leave on a windowsill, but out of direct sunlight.

04 When roots have formed, remove the cuttings from the water and insert them into gritty compost to continue growing.

Hack 24
Take hardwood rose cuttings

There are many different types of roses including floribundas, climbing, rambling, species, and hybrid tea types. One thing they all have in common is that it is fairly easy to take cuttings from them.

The easiest time to take a cutting is winter, when the new shoots from the previous season have turned woody. Look for a young, healthy shoot that is free from damage, pests, and diseases. Cut a 25cm (10in) length and trim it at the base to just below a bud.

Make a sloping cut at the top end just above a bud and pointing away from the bud. This ensures that when rain falls on the shoot it will drain away and not flow onto the top bud, which could cause it to rot.

Insert half the length of the hardwood rose cutting into a pot of general-purpose compost, or even directly into the soil. In spring you should notice new shoots emerging, rewarding you with a lovely new rose bush. Plant the bush out in your garden, or grow it on in a larger container.

Hack 25
Vertical strawberry planter

Strawberries look beautiful cascading down upright structures. This pallet hack means you can grow them vertically in just a tiny space. If you have a number of these vertical pallets, you can even use them to divide a garden or as a low fence.

Lay your pallet on the ground and remove every other slat from the front (I use a crowbar to do this) to create space for the plants to grow in. Flip the pallet over and lay landscape fabric (also called weed membrane) across the back. You'll need double the length of the pallet in landscape fabric, as you'll need the excess to create planting pockets. Cut the fabric vertically down the middle.

Use a staple gun to attach the landscape fabric all the way around the inside of the pallet. Then staple across the fabric by each slat, pushing the excess fabric through to create individual planting pockets. Now turn the pallet upright so that it is vertical. Fill the planting pockets with compost and plant your strawberries.

You will need

- Pallet
- Crowbar
- Landscape fabric
- Staple gun
- Strawberry plants

GROW

Hack 26
Grow early peas in gutters

One of my favourite hacks for getting an early crop of peas is to sow them in guttering. This is useful if your soil is heavy, because it will be cold and damp in spring, making germination hard. In gutters, you can use a compost of your choice.

Drill drainage holes every 8cm (3in) along the centre of a length of plastic guttering. I use about 2m (6ft). Fill the gutter with a general-purpose, peat-free compost to just below the top. Use a dibber or your finger to create 2cm (¾in) holes to sow the peas into. I sow them in a zigzag pattern along the centre of the gutter. Pop a pea seed into each hole and brush back the compost to cover, then water.

Once the peas are 12cm (5in) high they can be planted out. Use a hoe to create a shallow groove in the soil, about the same size as the gutter. Slide out the peas from the gutter into the groove – it should hold if the roots have established. Firm in and water.

Climbing frame

Peas are climbers, so they will need a structure to scramble up. I like to cut twiggy bits of hazel and insert them at intervals along the row next to the plants, and let the peas climb their way up. You can also stretch 1m (3ft) netting along the row, attached to posts at each end.

Free gourmet treat

Pea shoots are expensive to buy. I like to pinch out the tips when they reach 20cm (8in) high, removing 6cm (2½in) of growth, and add them to my salads. The remaining plant should give you more peas, because pinching out will encourage it to become more productive.

Hack 27
White pebbles for ripening fruit

One technique I learned when studying viticulture (growing grapevines), before I studied horticulture, was that vineyard growers often place white rocks, stones, or lumps of chalk under their vines to hasten the ripening of the grapes.

Lots of the vineyards I've visited in France use this technique. The theory is that the sunlight reflecting off the white surface increases the amount of available light and therefore speeds up the fruits' ripening. I pinched this idea to help some of the fruit trees in my garden. I place white pebbles on the surface of the root ball of many of my apple trees, plum trees, tomatoes, aubergines, and grapevines that I grow in pots. Not only does it speed up the ripening, but the stones also act as a mulch, helping to suppress weeds and retain moisture.

Hack 28
Grow a cactus from dragon fruit

If you like plants that are a bit quirky, here is a great example. Growing a dragon fruit from seed is easy and will reward you with a beautiful yet strange-looking cactus that makes a great houseplant.

All you need is a dragon fruit and a pot of compost. Follow the steps opposite and after a few weeks you'll see lots of tiny seedlings emerging. You can either carefully prick these individual seedlings out and grow them on as individual plants, or grow them as one tangled mass of cactus. I quite like the latter option. They are fairly slow growing and I've potted up the cactus into larger containers as they've got bigger. Dragon fruits are tropical plants, so you will have to keep them indoors unless you live somewhere very warm.

Colourful treat

You can buy the seeds (*Selenicereus undatus*) in a packet, but I like to buy the fruit as I enjoy eating it, before saving some of the seeds. You can find them in large supermarkets or Asian grocery stores. They come in a range of colours including red, pink, white, and yellow, so you can take your pick.

how to grow a prickly plant

01 Cut your dragon fruit in half with a knife. You will see loads of tiny black specks in the flesh.

02 Scoop a few of these seeds onto a plate. Let the seeds dry out for a few hours, to allow some of the flesh to evaporate.

03 Sprinkle the seeds over some compost in a pot and place it on a sunny windowsill.

04 Grow lots of individual seedlings together in one pot to create a quirky cactus to keep indoors.

Hack 29
Grow carrots for flowers

Carrots are biennial, meaning that they live for two years. Most people treat them as annuals by harvesting their delicious orange, and sometimes purple, yellow, black, and white roots in their first year.

My tip is to leave just a few carrots in the ground in the first year they are grown. After they have spent the subsequent winter chilling (the posh word for this is vernalization), they will produce spectacular flowers in the second summer. The blooms are similar to the wild flowers you might have seen in the countryside, only even more impressive. These carrot flowers are wonderful for attracting pollinators, which should increase yields of your surrounding crops.

Hack 30
Hose and rake seed driller

Drills are shallow grooves in the soil into which seeds can be sown directly. It can be quite laborious if you have to create a few rows of drills, as well as being tricky to get them in a straight line. Here is a hack to help.

For this hack you need very little except a large landscape rake (with a straight head, not one that fans out) and an old garden hose you don't mind cutting up. You can adjust the distance between the rows of drills (because different vegetable crops have different spacing requirements) by omitting putting the hose on some of the tines (see step 2).

how to make a seed driller

01 Use secateurs to cut some lengths of old garden hose that are slightly longer than the tines of a large rake.

02 Push the cut hose sections onto the tines at regular intervals.

03 Pull the rake firmly through the soil where you want to sow seed, and it will leave multiple rows of seed drills in its wake.

04 Sow your seeds by hand or using a pipe (see p.13), and water well.

Hack 31
Make a trug from sticks

It's amazing what you can make with just a few sticks. I made a trug and hanging basket out of old sticks, and it was one of my most popular videos on social media. It looks lovely and rustic and cost me practically nothing.

Take two sticks (about 45cm/18in long and 1cm/½in in diameter) and two lengths of string. The sticks and pieces of string should be roughly the same length. Tie them together to form a square, with two opposite sides being string and the other two sides being the two sticks.

Lay the structure on a table and then twist one stick over so that the strings cross in the middle and form an X shape. Start to thread more sticks under the string and with each end sitting on the two sticks forming the sides. Have the first stick at one end of your frame, and put the second at the other end. Continue to thread sticks under the string, alternating from side to side. As you fill the space, a domed shape will appear. Eventually you will run out of space under the string. You will just about be able to slot the last few sticks in place.

Trim the ends of your sticks so that they look neat and make a nice trug or basket shape. Tie string across the top to create a handle for a trug. If you want to make a hanging basket, secure several strings of your desired length to hang it from. Fill your trug or hanging basket with compost and plant or sow seeds into it.

You will need

+ Old sticks
+ String
+ Secateurs to cut your sticks and string to size

Hack 32
Tool unit from a pallet

The closest I get to storing tools in my shed is to bundle them all in at the end of the day and try to shut the door. However, it doesn't have to be like this. It is quite easy to make a storage unit from a pallet, which will keep your tools orderly and make your shed far less cluttered.

The easiest method is to take a pallet and remove one short side piece. Hold it with the remaining side piece sitting on the ground and the slats facing you. Attach it to the shed wall using brackets and screws and you have created a shallow, open-topped storage box perfect for your long-handled tools such as hoes, rakes, shovels, spades, forks, and brooms.

You can also make a storage solution for your hand tools. Remove the back of the pallet, including the chunky blocks, to make it much lighter, and then paint the remainder to make it look smart. Attach nails or hooks to hang trowels, dibbers, secateurs, and hand forks on. I've also made shelves to keep my seeds and surplus pots on, and attached boxes and recycled tins to keep nails, screws, and other small items in.

Pallet know-how

Recycled pallets are usually easy to find. Make sure you use pressure- or heat-treated pallets and not those treated with chemicals, which you don't want leaching into your soil. Look for a logo on the pallet – in the UK it will say HT for heat treated.

Hack 33
Mesh potato tower

Potatoes can take up a lot of space, so why not grow them vertically? Harvest the top layer first, keeping the remaining tower intact, then take the next layer of potatoes when needed.

You will need

+ Chicken wire or other metal mesh, 1.5m (5ft) wide
+ Wire cutters or secateurs
+ String
+ Garden compost
+ Potatoes

how to make a potato tower

01 Cut a 1.5m (5ft) length of chicken wire using wire cutters. You can use secateurs to cut the wire, but be careful not to damage them (see p.79).

02 Shape the chicken wire into a cylinder and tie the ends together with string or wire to prevent it unrolling.

03 Place the cylinder upright on the ground or even on the lawn. Add 25cm (10in) garden compost to the bottom of the tower.

04 Place four potatoes, equally spaced, on the surface. Cover over with 25cm (10in) more compost.

05 Place four more potatoes on the surface and again, cover with 25cm (10in) compost. Repeat until you've reached the top of the tower.

06 Potato shoots will start to grow through the sides, seeking out the light. After flowering you can start to harvest the potatoes.

Hack 34
Fork handle dibber

If a spade or fork happens to break while you are cultivating the garden, save it instead of throwing it away.

The handle part of your tool makes a great dibber for making planting holes, as shown below. If I have smaller seeds to sow, I use the end of a pencil, biro, or a bamboo cane to make narrower holes. If you buy a small dibber, it may come with a widger, which is a tool used to gently lever out tiny seedlings (pricking out). I often use a teaspoon for that job.

how to make a handy dibber

01 Use a sturdy knife to trim the end of the snapped-off fork handle into a blunt point.

02 Use the dibber to create holes in your vegetable beds. I use mine for planting out garlic, leeks, and potatoes in the spring.

GROW

Hack 35
Rake head storage

If you break the handle of a rake, repurpose it as a simple tool store. Like your broken hand tool, it can be given a second life. A rake head makes a simple storage solution to hang your hand tools on, as many trowels, hand forks, and other implements come with a hanging loop. Or uou can prop tools between the prongs.

how to keep your tools tidy

01 The simplest way to use your rake is to prop it against a garden wall or shed. You can hang tools from it or nestle them between the tines.

02 You can also screw the rake head to a shed wall and then suspend your tools from its prongs.

Hack 36
Store hand tools in sand

Hand tools can end up getting rusty if they aren't stored correctly after use. One of my favourite hacks is to store them in a bucket of sand with just a dollop of engine oil added.

After using your hand tools such as trowels, wipe the metal surfaces with an oily rag. Fill a bucket almost to the top with sand. Add some engine oil – just enough to make the sand ever so slightly moist.

Push the hand tools into the sand so that just the metal sections are covered. Open the blades on tools such as secateurs and pliers before putting them into the sand. Leave the tools in the sand until you are ready to use them again, wiping off the sand with your oily rag before using.

The sand and oil mix shouldn't need changing for a good few months and will keep your hand tools lovely and clean as well as rust-free. The oil prevents the tools becoming rusty, while the abrasive qualities of the sand means they are easy to brush down and clean, preventing the metal oxidizing and becoming rusty in the first place.

Hacks 37–42
Slugs and snails

Every gardener knows these molluscs can rapidly wipe out seedlings or young plants (sometimes overnight).

The next few hacks are a few of my favourites to keep them at bay, and avoid the disappointment of inspecting your plants in the morning and discovering there is virtually nothing left.

Hedgehog home

Hedgehogs eat a range of different foods but they are predominantly insectivores and feed off many of the bugs found in your garden, including slugs. Encourage them in and you will gain a natural predator ready to reduce slug damage to your garden. Ready-made hedgehog homes can be expensive. Instead, select a medium-sized plastic or terracotta pot and lay it on its side. Position it in a shady, out-of-the-way corner such as behind a shed or under a hedge. Half-fill the pot with dried leaves or dried grass. You can partially screen the opening with a stone or brick to make it more cosy, but leave at least a 15cm (6in) gap for a hedgehog to crawl in. Try not to be inquisitive and keep checking the pot as a hedgehog will quickly move out if it feels vulnerable. Instead, try sitting outside quietly in the evening with a cup of tea and see if you can spot a hedgehog snuffling its way across your garden looking for food including, hopefully, your slugs.

Salt to banish slugs

I love this trick as it is so simple and easy. I wrap double-sided sticky tape around the bottom of a plant pot and then roll it in salt. The salt should stick to the tape and act as a barrier, preventing slugs and snails climbing up the sides of your pots. You can also wrap the tape around a seedling tray – I do this with lots of my seedlings. When watering your plants, be careful not to get water on the tape as it will wash away the salt, rending the tape ineffective. And don't get salt directly on the compost or plants, as it can harm the plants.

Sheep's wool repeller

One of my favourite finds on country walks is sheep's wool. I often find it attached to fences or barbed wire where the sheep have rubbed or snagged themselves. I collect the wool and bring it home to use in my garden. Slugs and snails hate walking across the wool fibres as it irritates the large "foot" that they travel on. Wool is also coarse and dry, which slugs don't like, preferring moister surfaces. For this reason, I lay wool over the compost in my pots and hanging baskets and put it around the edges of my seed trays. I've found it is one of the most effective methods of protecting my plants from them. Another benefit of using wool on the surface of the soil is that it makes an excellent natural mulch. It helps retain moisture as well as preventing weeds from germinating. If you can't gather wool yourself, bags of wool are sold online and in garden centres to use as described above, both as a mulch and to keep slugs and snails at bay.

Walk the plank

Another method I've found to be effective against slugs is to lean a plank of wood against a raised bed in the evening, on the shadiest side. If conditions are dry, wet it slightly. In the morning you will find loads of slugs and snails have congregated on the underside of the plank. You simply need to pick them off the plank and dispose of them.

PROTECT

Beer traps

Some people feel that the ideal way to depart this world is this hack: drowning in beer. Joking aside, slugs and snails love beer's yeasty, sugary smell and will often be enticed towards it. Gardeners can use the aroma to catch them.

To make a beer trap for snails and slugs, find a shallow terracotta or glass dish or a jam jar. Dig a small hole in the ground near the plants that you want to protect. The hole needs to be just as wide as the dish, but slightly shallower. Sit your dish into the hole so that the rim sits just proud of the ground by a couple of centimetres. This is to ensure that other insects such as ground beetles don't accidentally fall into the beer.

Finally, pour in a glug of beer. When you return in the morning you will be amazed to see how many slugs and snails have fallen into the trap and drowned. You can then tip the slugs onto the ground to allow local wildlife such as the birds and hedgehogs to enjoy them.

Copper

Slugs and snails also hate copper. When their "slime" comes into contact with copper, it causes a mild electric pulse that is uncomfortable. You can use copper strips around pots in the same way as salt. The slugs and snails dislike crossing the copper. Copper strips are readily available and you can cut them to size.

Hack 43
Ladybird hotel against aphids

Ladybird larvae are voracious hunters of aphids, which will help reduce potential plant damage. This hack welcomes them to your garden.

One of the easiest ways of attracting ladybirds is to grow a range of nectar- and pollen-rich flowering plants (see box). Another method is to collect a few hollow canes such as bamboo or pampas grass, or even a bundle of dried grass, and shove them into a flowerpot. The pot is now a ladybird hotel. Lay it on its side and leave it somewhere sheltered such as beside a shed, and soon the ladybirds will move in and start to breed.

Pollen-rich plants

Ladybirds love flowers from the carrot family with their large umbel-shaped heads. These include edibles such as parsley, celery, fennel, dill, parsnips, and carrots of course. The flat flowerheads of the daisy family, such as cosmos, marigold, and yarrow also provide a nice landing pad for ladybirds and other pollinators.

Hack 44
Sticky tape against blackfly

Blackfly are small aphids that feed on the sap of your plants. They can cause leaves and shoots to shrivel and die, and you may need to take steps to control them.

This is a quick and easy method. You will very often see blackfly on the underside of leaves or on newly growing stems. One of my favourite hacks is to wrap sticky tape around my fingers, with the sticky side on the outside. Then I rub my fingers up and down the affected stems. The blackfly should stick to the sticky tape and come away from the plant.

Hack 45
Feather and potato bird scarer

Who would have thought a potato and a few feathers could be scary? Perhaps not to us gardeners, but combine them into a bird scarer and it will deter birds from eating your crops.

Apparently, this is an ancient method for saving your fruit and veg from birds, and is even said to have been associated with witchcraft and magic. In reality, if you hang a potato covered in feathers above your crops, pretending it's a large, scary bird, it's bound to act as a deterrent.

Finding your feathers

Please don't go and pluck an innocent living bird for this! You can usually find feathers easily enough on the ground. I live near the sea in Southern England and I'm always finding seagull feathers. But if you don't live in a coastal location, you can usually find feathers on walks in both the countryside or in urban environments, such as under buildings where pigeons have been roosting. If you live near a park with a lake, there are usually hundreds of feathers on the surrounding area and banks where water fowl such as geese, swans, and ducks have been sitting.

how to make your feathered demon

01 Find a large potato and use a skewer to create a hole through the middle.

02 Thread some string through the hole, which you'll use to hang your feathered demon above the crops.

03 Push a feather into the potato; the quill ends should be sharp enough to stick securely.

PROTECT

04 Continue inserting feathers into the potato until it looks a bit like a bird – if you scrunched your eyes up and had a good imagination! Then hang it somewhere above or beside your plants.

Crop protector

The feathered potato will move and dance in the wind and hopefully deter real birds from eating your crops.

Hack 46
Milk against mildew

Courgettes are almost too easy to grow. Most years they will reward you with a glut. However, they are really susceptible to powdery mildew, which strikes when the roots become dry. My hack seems to work on other plants infected with powdery mildew, including begonias, cucumbers, squashes, and grapevines. Why not give it a try?

Powdery mildew looks as though somebody has sprinkled icing sugar all over the leaves. This fungus spreads rapidly and, if not treated, the leaves will quickly shrivel and the plant will die. Mix one part milk with two parts water in a spray bottle. At the first sign of powdery mildew, remove the infected leaves and spray the remainder, including the underside of the leaves, with the milk and water. I've heard gardeners say that this is more effective done on a sunny day, too. Do remember to water around the roots of the courgettes regularly to prevent them drying out and becoming susceptible again.

There are various theories why the milk and water prevents powdery mildew. It may create a film on the leaves to prevents the mildew spores spreading, or the milk may alter the pH of the leaves, discouraging the mildew. Whatever the reason, it does seem to be effective.

PROTECT

Hack 47
Rotate your veg crops

Rotating crops means changing where you grow your veg annually, so that nothing grows in the same location year after year.

The theory is that many pests and diseases remain in the soil the following year after they developed. Moving crops means fewer problems; a pest or fungus may fade or die because their host plants are no longer there. Another benefit is that you'll avoid depleting the soil and give it a chance to recover as it grows a different plant.

Crop rotation is designed for annual vegetable crops; perennial crops such as asparagus or rhubarb stay in the ground for more than one year. Most growers categorize their annual veg into three groups, below. (Other veggies such as tomatoes and courgettes can be slotted into any spare spaces.)

Legumes Including all peas and beans.
Brassicas The cabbage family including kale, broccoli, cauliflower, and kohlrabi.
Roots and potatoes Most plants that produce an edible root such as carrots, parsnips, and beetroot.

If you start with potatoes and roots in bed one, they will break up the soil and make a nice deep root run for peas and beans. The roots of the beans and peas fix nitrogen in the soil, increasing its fertility. This makes it suitable in the third year for brassicas, which are more demanding of nutrients. Follow the plan in the box to get started.

First year
Bed 1 Potatoes and roots
Bed 2 Brassicas
Bed 3 Legumes

Second year
Bed 1 Legumes
Bed 2 Potatoes and roots
Bed 3 Brassicas

Third year
Bed 1 Brassicas
Bed 2 Legumes
Bed 3 Potatoes and roots

Hack 48
Spice jar eye protectors

Gardening is so rewarding, but there are times when you need to take extra care. One of the most common accidents in the garden is bending down, when weeding, or planting, and catching your eye on the end of a sharp bamboo cane.

The best method of avoiding an eye accident is to cover the sharp end of a bamboo cane with something blunt. You can buy eye-protector caps to place over the protruding end to avoid such a nasty occurrence, but there are household items you can recycle, which work just as well.

My favourite choice is recycling small spice jars. They don't weigh too much, yet are heavy enough not to blow away in strong gusts of winds. You can also use milk cartons or larger jam jars, or cut the tops off plastic bottles and place them over the cane ends. I've even known people with clay soil in their garden who shape or mould small soil balls and push them onto the canes.

My favourite eye-safety hack – because I love playing tennis – is to recycle old tennis balls. I carefully make a hole in some old balls and push them onto the end of canes.

Hack 49
Decoy strawberries

Just like us, birds love strawberries. It can be very frustrating to anticipate snacking on your ripening fruit, only to find the birds have got there first.

Larger birds often take whole berries, while smaller ones peck holes in them. A great hack is to collect small pebbles, a similar size to a strawberry, and paint them red. Place a few around your strawberry plants as the fruits start to ripen. The idea is that the birds will initially peck at these red stones, discover they are inedible, and therefore not bother eating the real thing when they turn the same colour.

PROTECT

Hack 50
Spicy bird seed

Squirrels may look cute, but they are less appealing when eating the food you put out for the birds. Try a few (wildlife-friendly) hacks to deter them.

Stop squirrels stealing seed from bird feeders by mixing chilli powder or cayenne with the seed. You only need a sprinkle, but you may need to experiment with the quantity. The squirrels hate it, and after one taste will quickly disappear, with luck never to return. Birds don't seem to notice the chilli, as they have very few taste buds. Before you know it, they will happily flock (pun intended) to your feeder.

Slippery customer

If you have a bird feeder attached to an upright pole, you might find this keeps squirrels at bay. Grease the pole with some petroleum jelly and the squirrels won't be able to climb up it. However, do keep the grease away from areas that birds are feeding on, as it won't be good for their feathers if they were to come into contact with it.

Hack 51
Flowerpot earwig catchers

If you've ever grown dahlias (see box), you may have noticed that some of the blooms become raggedy at the edges. This is often caused by earwigs, which love to **nibble the edges of the flowers**. Don't despair – there is a simple solution and it costs nothing.

Stuff a small flowerpot with dried grass or straw. Push a bamboo cane into the ground next to your dahlia, or any flower you wish to protect, then turn your pot upside-down and pop it on the end. The theory is that earwigs will crawl into the inverted pot overnight for shelter. All you need to do is pick up the pot first thing in the morning and shake the contents elsewhere in the garden, and you should see lots of earwigs drop out. If you have an apple tree in your garden drop them there, as earwigs are helpful in eating other insects that are pests in orchards.

Dahlia dauphinois

Did you know you can eat your home-grown dahlia tubers? Wash well and peel, then fry or boil them as you would potatoes. Make sure they have grown for a year in your garden first, as dahlias are sometimes treated with chemicals and this will "detox" them.

Hack 52
Container bulb saver

Try this hack to stop squirrels digging up bulbs from all your lovingly planted pots.

You will need
- Chicken wire
- Wire cutters or secateurs
- Tent pegs (optional)
- Compost

how to squirrel-proof your pots

01 Plant your bulbs in pots in the usual way.

02 Place a sheet of chicken wire over them immediately after planting, and cut to fit the surface of your pot using wire cutters or secateurs.

03 If you use secateurs to cut the wire, be careful not to damage them.

04 If you look at the base of the blade you'll spot a small notch. Use that to cut through the wire, rather than the blade.

05 Press the wire down. You can use tent pegs to hold the chicken wire in place, although I find the weight of the top compost is enough.

06 Cover the wire with 2cm (¾in) compost. The bulbs find their way through, so there's no need to remove the chicken wire as they grow.

Hack 53
Catmint to divert cats

While many of us adore our feline friends, cats can be a nuisance if they are using your flowerbeds as a public convenience. It might not even be your cat, but a neighbour's moggy who likes to pop over the fence whenever nature calls. This is my favourite trick to deter them.

My hack to prevent cats from using your garden as a toilet is to plant catmint, also known as catnip or nepeta. This might feel counterintuitive because cats love this plant, but if they are coming into your garden anyway, this is a great way of diverting them away from your favourite flowers or seating areas. Plant the nepeta in a neglected corner of your garden. It will act like a magnet to cats, which will be drawn to that area and stay away from your ornamental and edible plants.

PROTECT

Hack 54
Companion planting

Plants often benefit from each other's company, if grown closely together. It's a bit like grouping your plants into pairs of friends. Sometimes one attracts pests away from the other; sometimes one plant attracts pollinators. Their growing habits may be mutually beneficial, such as in the three sisters (see p.166). Here are some companions that work effectively in my garden.

Marigolds near tomatoes
Tomatoes often suffer from infestations of whitefly, particularly in the greenhouse. If you grow French marigolds near the tomatoes, the whitefly are lured over to these pretty yellow, orange, and red flowers and stay off your ripening fruits. And the marigolds look great.

Alliums near carrots
Carrots can suffer from carrot root fly, which burrow in and make them inedible. However, the pungent aroma of onions, chives, or leeks growing nearby seems to distract these minibeasts. The powerful smell of mint is also said to confuse carrot root fly and keep them away from your carrots.

Nasturtiums near cabbages
Cabbage white butterflies can quickly destroy your crop of brassicas, but if you plant nasturtiums near your cabbages you might find that the butterflies lay their eggs on this gorgeous flowering plant instead.

PROTECT

Hack 55
De-weed your patio

Some weeds in the garden can be good for wildlife, but too many will compete for nutrients, light, and water with the plants you want to grow. Instead of reaching for a bottle of weed killer, I simply put the kettle on.

A weed is a plant in the wrong place. And although many weeds can be beneficial for the garden, there are an awful lot more that are unsightly and in exactly the spot that you don't want them.

I take my kettle outside and pour the freshly boiled water over weeds. This works best on plants growing up through the patio or on gravel. The boiling water kills the leaves of the plants. It is a great method for killing off annual weeds such as fat hen and chickweed. Some perennial types such as dandelion, nettle, and docks might require more than one application of boiling water. Be careful not to splash the boiling water on any of your nearby plants.

Do note that boiling water probably won't work for more pernicious weeds such as bindweed, Japanese knotweed, and ground elder, and you'll need to find harsher or more radical treatments to control those. But boiling water is useful as a quick treatment for controlling many of the common weeds on your patio or in your garden that are preventing your plants from growing properly.

Hack 56
Free liquid plant food

Why buy expensive fertilizers when it's easy to make your own liquid plant food? You probably have the ingredients in your garden already. The two most popular are comfrey and nettles, both common "weeds" often found growing in your garden or in the countryside.

Liquid comfrey feed is higher in potassium, which is needed by plants predominantly to help increase flowering, produce fruit, and develop colour and flavour. Nettle feed, on the other hand, is higher in nitrogen, which boosts green growth and helps the plant establish. I generally feed my plants with liquid nettle feed in spring, when the plants are getting going and need a boost. As the plants start to form flowers and fruit, I switch to comfrey feed to improve fruit set and colour.

You make liquid nettle and comfrey feed in exactly the same way. Just remember to wear gloves when harvesting the nettles to avoid getting stung.

You will need
- Secateurs or scissors
- Nettles or comfrey
- Bucket
- Large plastic containers

how to brew nettle fertilizer

01 Use secateurs or scissors to cut freshly grown nettles. The best time to do this is in spring, when they are making lots of lush new growth and before they start flowering.

02 Chop the nettles into smallish pieces. This helps them break down and decompose faster.

03 Put the nettles into a bucket and then top it up with water so they are covered.

04 If the nettles float to the top, put a brick on top to keep them submerged. Leave the bucket somewhere out of the way, such as at the end of the garden. This is because the liquid can really stink when the nettles start to rot down. After a few weeks your concentrated liquid feed should be ready to use.

05 I pour mine into recycled plastic bottles to store until needed. To use the liquid fertilizer, mix 1 part feed to 10 parts water in a watering can. I give it a stir with a stick or short bit of bamboo cane. Use this diluted liquid feed once a week during the growing season by watering around the roots of your plants.

Cultivate comfrey

Make comfrey fertilizer the same way. If there is no comfrey growing wild nearby, it is easy to grow from root cuttings from a friend. Dig up a clump to reveal the root and plant a 5cm (2in) section in your own garden. They grow quite quickly and soon you'll have an established patch to give you a constant supply.

Hack 57
Two-bucket wormery

Not all of us have room for a compost heap (although some ready-made composters are fairly compact). Why not try making a wormery from old plastic buckets instead? Some people even keep one under the kitchen sink. Amazingly, they don't seem to smell at all.

Use a drill to create lots of holes around the outside of one bucket (which has a lid) so the worms can breathe. Avoid drilling holes in the lid if you intend to keep the wormery outside, as it will fill with rainwater. It's fine to do this if you're keeping the wormery indoors. You also need to drill holes in the base. This will be your top bucket.

Place two bricks in the other bucket and sit the top bucket on them. This will allow air to circulate and prevent the top bucket sitting in worm leachate when it starts to collect. Add a base of shredded paper to the top bucket, followed by a layer of organic matter such as garden compost or soil.

Next, add worms to the top bucket. You need compost worms such as red or tiger worms. You can often find them in the garden under stones or rocks, or in an existing compost heap, or you can buy them online. Don't use earthworms.

Put the lid on the top bucket. Ideally the wormery should be kept at a temperature of 5–20°C (41–68°F) and in the shade. If you're keeping it outside, move it into a shed over winter.

Add kitchen scraps (see p.96 for what to include), to feed the worms. If everything feels dry, water it a little, as worms prefer slightly moist conditions. Check the bottom bucket regularly and tip out the leachate (see box) to use as a plant feed.

You will need

- Drill
- 2 plastic containers or buckets, 1 with a lid
- 2 bricks
- Shredded paper
- Compost or soil
- Compost worms

Free plant food

Wormeries not only take up little space, but the worms will also break down kitchen waste and make it into compost. You can also collect the liquid that collects in the bottom container, sometimes called worm leachate, to use as a rich liquid plant food. Simply dilute 1 part leachate to 10 parts water.

Hack 58
Make leaf mould

There is almost nothing more desirable to a gardener than free compost. One type of compost that gardeners love is called leaf mould, and it is made from rotted leaves. Although it is generally low in nutrients, leaf mould can be used in potting mixes in containers or as a soil conditioner and improver.

In autumn, there is an abundance of fallen leaves, which you can collect and let rot down to become leaf mould. Rake leaves into piles and tip them into old bin liners or compost bags, poke some holes in the bottom to let any excess moisture drain away, and then leave them somewhere out of sight and forget about them for a year or so. When you come back to them, you should have beautiful, friable leaf mould to use in the garden. I like to spread it under trees as a mulch, mimicking the natural conditions of a woodland, and as a mulch for my vegetable beds over winter. Take care not to tidy up all the leaves from your garden. Leave plenty for wildlife, as many species will use them for nesting and hibernation.

Scoop for success

Use two small planks – one in each hand – to scoop up lots of fallen leaves. You'll pick up much more like that than with your hands or using a rake or spade.

Mower power

Before bagging your autumn leaves, run your rotary mower over them, using the box on the back of the mower to collect them. Then tip them into a bag. The mower will have chopped the leaves into smaller pieces, making them decompose much faster than uncut leaves.

Hack 59
Mole hill magic

For some people, spotting mole hills on their precious lawns is one of their biggest horticultural fears. However, apart from looking unsightly, moles and their hills do very little damage to our gardens, and the mini mounds that moles make can be put to good use in the potting shed.

As they say, every cloud has a silver lining, and I rejoice when I see mole hills in the garden. The mound of soil can be scooped into a bucket with a trowel and used as a wonderful potting mix. It is usually lovely and friable, as the moles have done a great job in breaking up any clods of soil into smaller crumbs as they create their tunnels underground. I use it for potting up my plants and for sowing into. You can also use mole hills to fill raised beds or containers. It's a completely free resource and cheaper than buying potting compost from the garden centre. It's also sustainable, as there are zero miles involved in collecting it from your garden.

NURTURE

Hack 60
Potassium power

This is another hack that uses something you might otherwise throw away. Next time you are sweeping the fireplace, save some ashes for the garden.

If you have a log fire or a log-burning stove, you can use wood ash (potash) to feed your plants. Avoid using ash from coal and charcoal. Collect the wood ash when it is cold and sprinkle it around the root area of trees and shrubs. I use wood ash around my fruit trees as it is high in potassium, which promotes better flowering, colour, and flavour of the berries.

Compost booster

You can also add wood ash to compost occasionally – but add it too often and it will make your soil more alkaline. For this reason, avoid placing it around acid-loving plants such as blueberries, cranberries, heathers, and rhododendrons

Hack 61
Space-saving composting

If you don't have room for a compost bin in your garden but still want to recycle your kitchen and garden waste, I have a handy solution. You can simply bury it all in the ground and leave it to decompose.

There are many benefits to burying organic materials in the soil instead of using a compost bin. It's a real space-saver (I keep my scraps in a bucket under the kitchen sink), and you don't have to put up with an unsightly composting area in your garden. You save time and effort, too, as you don't need to spend your weekends turning over the compost. Simply bury it, forget about it for a few months, and let the worms do the work for you.

When your scraps have decomposed (see step 3), dig up the compost and use it for potting up plants. Even easier, just leave the compost where it is and plant a tree or shrub on the spot. It will enjoy the nutrient-rich growing conditions.

Add to your soil
- Vegetable waste
- Old leaves
- Herbaceous plant material
- Grass clippings
- Cardboard and paper
- Wood ash from a bonfire

Avoid these!
- Dairy, fish, and meat leftovers
- Dog poo
- Magazines and glossy paper
- Cooking oils
- Ash from a coal fire

how to slow-cook your compost

01 Collect compostable kitchen waste (see "Add to your soil" opposite). When your scraps bin is full, take it outside and dig a hole in a vegetable bed. The size will depend on how much material you have; I usually dig a hole 30–40cm (12–16in) deep.

02 Tip your scraps into the hole and cover it over with the soil you just dug up.

03 If you are concerned that rodents or other wildlife might dig it up, cover it with a patio slab or sheet of timber and weigh it down. Later on in the year (give it a few months), return to the hole and remove the patio slab. You will discover that your kitchen waste has decomposed and been transformed into compost.

Hack 62
Compost bin rat repeller

Many people are put off having a compost bin because they fear it will attract rats. Avoiding adding meat, fish, and dairy products makes it less likely they will visit but, unfortunately, they can still come looking for vegetable peelings or fruit and seed scraps.

If you have a Dalek-type compost bin, despite its hard plastic exterior and lid, rats often tunnel into the soil underneath the bin and then up inside. To prevent this happening you can place the bin on patio slabs.

However, compost bins work best if they are sitting directly on soil, allowing worms to move up into the bin, which speeds up the decomposition of the material. To stop rats tunnelling underneath but allow worms in, sit the compost bin on a strip of fine-meshed chicken wire. Staple the wire to the sides, too. This will ensure rats can't get into the bin, and with luck they'll go elsewhere for their food.

Acid effect

Onion scraps and citrus peels can be very acidic, which affects the decomposition of the compost heap, so add them in moderation. Rats can potentially spread harmful bacteria such as E. coli and salmonella so check the list on p.96 for what to keep out of your bin.

NURTURE

Hack 63
Chop your compost

Gardeners love compost – it enriches the soil and boosts plant growth. You can never have enough. Here's a quick hack to accelerate the process.

Composting depends on organic material decomposing. However, it can seem to take forever before you end up with the lovely, friable brown stuff that our soil and plants love so much. Speed up the process by chopping up the material as small as possible. I've even seen gardeners putting their electric brush cutters into compost bins to break down herbaceous material! So, next time you're adding material to your compost heap, grab your secateurs and get chopping.

Hack 64
Recycled pallet compost bay

I always think that if you want to start gardening, then begin with a compost heap. Once you've got the compost established you can use it to mulch your borders and plant into it. And a compost heap is a great way to reduce both garden and kitchen waste, saving it from landfill.

You can of course buy composters, but it is very easy to make them by recycling old pallets. You'll need to find heat-treated pallets (see p.51).

To make one compost bin you will need three pallets, one for the back and two for the sides. Simply lay the three pallets on edge with their corners butted up to create an open-fronted bay, then use brackets and screws to attach them together. I often just use wire to tie them together instead of brackets, which seems to hold all three pallets tightly enough together to create a sturdy compost bin. Then you simply need to add your compost material and leave it to decompose.

Hack 65
Colour your compost

Compost bins can sometimes get slimy, smelly, and attract flies if care isn't taken to ensure a good balance of green and brown material. Follow this quick guide to compost contentment.

Green material includes grass clippings, herbaceous materials, and fruit and vegetable scraps, which are usually high in nitrogen. It is nitrogen that causes compost to become slimy. To balance the green material you need to add brown materials, which are carbon based. These include newspaper, paper, wood chip, dry leaves, and cardboard. Aim for a 50:50 balance of green and brown material. This should prevent your compost from smelling.

Water it too

Water your compost heap a little if the texture feels too dry. If you have a compost bin with a lid, just leave the lid off when rain is predicted. You can also wee on your heap! Urine contains nutrients that plants require including nitrogen, potassium, and phosphorus.

NURTURE

Hack 66
Rotate your compost

It's always a good idea to turn a compost heap to add oxygen, which speeds up the decomposition of the organic matter. Not only does it speed up decomposition, but it is also a good workout.

Turning compost usually means using a fork to dig out the material from one compost bay and then putting it into another bay, or simply returning it to the same spot. Not all of us feel so energetic in the garden. Thankfully, there is an easier way to turn the soil. It involves purchasing a rotating composter (easily found online). These composters are drum-shaped with a handle and can be spun in either direction, which rotates and aerates the compost for you for minimum effort. It's far less physically demanding. I love using mine.

Hack 67
Banana skin plant food

Whether you buy them to eat, or grow these tropical plants for their architectural foliage, the ap-peel of bananas includes liquid fertilizer made from the skin, mulch provided by their large leaves, and using their gas to ripen fruit.

Banana peel is packed full of nutrients, particularly potassium, which helps plants grow. Instead of adding your banana skins to the compost heap, use them to make a potent liquid plant food. Your plants will love the extra nutrients and it will help them develop. If you don't fancy making a liquid feed, you can also chop up banana peel and either bury it in the garden or scatter it around fruit bushes and roses. The peel will gradually break down and act as a slow-release fertilizer.

Saved by the skin

If you're struggling to get green tomatoes to ripen, pop them into a paper bag with a banana and roll it closed. As the banana ripens it gives off a gas called ethene (also known as ethylene), which helps ripen surrounding fruit, including your tomatoes.

how to brew banana booster

01 After you've eaten your banana, chop the skin small with scissors.

02 Put the pieces in a jar of water and leave overnight.

03 Next morning, the water should be a murky brown colour.

04 Sieve the liquid and use it (no need to dilute) to feed your plants and give them a boost.

Hack 68
Coffee booster

What could be better after your morning coffee than a stroll round the garden to do some light watering?

After you've enjoyed your breakfast, leave the coffee grounds in the bottom of the cafetière. Fill it up to the top with water and then water your plants with the liquid. The coffee is packed with nutrients that plants need. However, too much coffee can make the soil slightly acidic, so do this infrequently for the majority of your plants. Exceptions are acidic-soil lovers such as blueberries, cranberries, rhododendrons, and camellias. Coffee is ideal for them.

NURTURE

Hack 69
Eggshell fertilizer

Don't throw out your eggshells. They are crammed with nutrients that plants require for growth, including calcium. Give this hack a try instead.

Give the shells a good rinse and blitz them in a food processor to a fine powder. Add the powder to your compost heap and mix it in. Alternatively, sprinkle it over your soil and rake it in. The calcium is released gradually, so add eggshell powder to your soil regularly to help plants grow over a few years.

Houseplant hack

You can also leave coffee granules to dry out, then lightly sprinkle them around your plants. I often do this with my houseplants, just like a granular fertilizer. Don't do this too often, though, as it can alter the pH of your soil.

Hack 70
Bindweed liquid feed

Bindweed can be made into a potent liquid, packed full of essential nutrients, which you can use to feed and super-charge your plants during the growing season, resulting in healthy leaves, more flowers, and more fruit.

Many of us will have experienced the dreaded sight of bindweed emerging in the garden. It is a very invasive climber that will smother neighbouring plants and eventually kill them. It's extremely hard to eradicate because if just a tiny part of the root is left in the ground, it will keep growing, coming back stronger than before.

Another difficulty is what to do with the plant material once it has been removed. If it is added to the compost, then the roots will quickly establish themselves and regrow. My solution is to make it into a liquid feed. If you drown bindweed roots in a bucket of water for a few weeks until they rot, the liquid retains nutrients that plants need to grow.

All types of plants will benefit from an occasional drink of this potent liquid feed. Note that plants only need feeding when they are growing, which is usually between early spring and late summer. There is no need to feed plants when they are dormant (typically late summer through to late winter).

how to make powerful liquid feed

01 Collect your bindweed roots and shoots and place them in a bucket of water. Ensure all the bindweed is completely submerged. Leave them to decompose and rot, which might take a few weeks.

02 Eventually the water will become brown and muddy. You now have a bindweed liquid feed concentrate, which you can bottle for storage.

03 To use the bindweed liquid feed, half-fill your watering can, add a glug of the bindweed feed, and then fill it up to the top with more water. Use a stick to stir it in well. Pour this around the roots of your plants once a week and watch them flourish.

Hack 71
Mulch your borders

If you want to reduce the amount of weeding you do, then covering over any bare soil or compost is a must. Gardeners refer to this as mulching, and it involves creating a layer of organic or non-organic matter on the ground.

The main reasons for mulching are to suppress weeds, help retain moisture in the soil, and help reduce soil erosion. Some organic mulches such as rotted horse manure, sheep's wool (see p.62), and garden compost can also add to the fertility of the soil by providing a few extra nutrients. Recycled wood chip and wood bark make good mulches for flowerbeds and borders. Organic matter will eventually break down into the soil, so will need topping up regularly.

Non-organic mulch options include pebbles, shells, gravel, and slate. I've even seen marbles used as a pretty decorative mulch.

Let weeds dry out

In hot weather, you can leave hoed weeds to decompose on the ground, as they will quickly desiccate in the hot sun. It will increase the organic matter in your soil and saves you having to pick them up and clear them away.

MAINTAIN

Hack 72
Perfect your lawn edges

Struggling to get a straight edge on your lawn? Try my nifty hack with an old plank of wood and your own body weight.

The traditional solution might be to tie the ends of a length of string to two small stakes and stretch it out so that the string pulls taut, along an area that you wish to mark out. But there is an even easier solution. Place a plank of wood on the edge of lawn you wish to be straight, and stand on top of it to hold it firm. Then use a half-moon tool to cut a sharp edge following the side of the plank. You'll have a perfectly straight edge to your flower border in no time.

Hack 73
No dig

Traditionally it was always good practice to dig over the soil in borders, vegetable patches, and flowerbeds. However, research shows that more often than not you're doing more damage than good. For this reason many gardeners are now practising "no dig" gardening.

"No dig" is exactly what it says: avoid digging and disturbing the soil. It is usually done in kitchen gardens and allotments for growing vegetables, but occasionally also used in herbaceous borders and ornamental flowerbeds.

There are numerous reasons why not digging is beneficial. It is far less work. Digging with a fork or spade can be onerous, and the no dig method is much quicker, more efficient, and avoids your back aching. Digging over the soil can destroy its structure, which is so essential for plants to grow well. When left undisturbed, the soil retains more fertility in the planting root zone (the top 10–15cm/4–6in for most veggies) and will hold on to moisture better during dry periods. No dig gardening is also beneficial if you are planting near large trees, where cultivating and digging into the soil may damage the roots.

Finally, digging exposes weed seeds that might otherwise have lain dormant in the ground. And you can inadvertently chop through perennial roots, such as dandelion and plantain, which end up spreading further. Every time you chop through a root, you multiply its opportunity to propagate and become yet another weed. Follow the steps over the page to be a no dig gardener.

how to create a no dig bed

01 First you need to cover the soil with cardboard. There is usually no need to dig out any weeds first, but if you have lots of tall weeds, you could strim or cut them down to ground level. Simply covering them with cardboard will keep them in the dark and stop them growing. For really persistent weeds, you can add two or three sheets of cardboard to create a stronger barrier.

02 Give the cardboard a good soak of water and then top it with a 10cm (4in) mulch of well-rotted garden compost and rake it level.

Knotty problem

This method is a wonderful way of controlling most annual and perennial weeds and reducing garden work. However, if you have really invasive weeds such as Japanese knotweed and horsetail, you will need to eradicate them before covering the soil with cardboard and compost.

03 Soak the cardboard and the compost to help them bind together. You are now ready to plant or sow your seeds into the soil.

Occasionally new seeds or older perennial seeds may grow, but the advantage of this method is that the compost is loose, making the weeds easy to pull out by hand. Often perennial roots won't snap, but come away easily in your hand.

04 If you stay on top of the weeds, and top up with compost and cardboard each year, you should end up with a bumper crop of vegetables. You will also have far less weeding and maintenance to do each season.

Hack 74
Coat hanger hoe

Did you know you can make a simple hoe from a coat hanger? It's a handy gadget for removing small annual weeds from your flower borders.

In the garden, pull the hoe lightly back and forth across and through annual weeds to slice through their roots. They aren't deep rooted and you should be able to pull them up with light pressure. Try to catch annual weeds in their early stages of growth, before they start producing seed. Otherwise, seeds will spill and germinate in the surrounding soil.

You will need

- Wire cutters
- Wire coat hanger
- Old broom handle or sturdy stick
- Hose or jubilee clip, or cable ties

how to turn a hanger into a hoe

01 Take your hanger and pull the centre of the long straight side down, shaping it to form an elongated diamond shape.

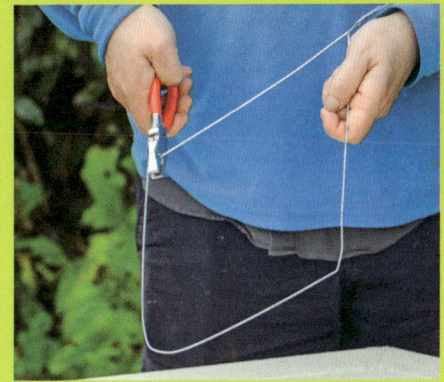

02 Using wire cutters, cut the hanging hook off the top of your coat hanger. Shape the wire into a rough hoe shape (see step 3).

03 Attach the cut ends of the wire coat hanger securely to the end of an old broom handle or stick. Use a hose clip, a cable tie or two, or even tight rubber bands.

04 The wire loop is now your cutting "blade" and your hoe is ready to use.

MAINTAIN

Hack 75
Collect rainwater

You can save loads of money on your water bill if you harvest rainwater. It's so easy to catch water in a water butt and, of course, it's completely free. And with climate change leading to heavier rainfall, there is an opportunity to collect gallons.

No longer will you need to attach a hosepipe to a mains water tap. Water butt kits with all the fixings to attach to your gutters and downpipes are readily available online or from local DIY stores. Sometimes local authorities even give away water butts to residents. Alternatively, it is easy enough to convert an old wheelie bin to collect rainwater (see box).

If you don't fancy rigging up a water butt, you can always leave buckets outside when it's raining to collect water, and save it to water your plants during a dry spell. At the very least, stick some of your hardier houseplants outside when it's raining to give them a drink. Don't forget to bring them back indoors afterwards!

Convert a wheelie bin

Drill a hole large enough to accommodate a water butt tap about 10cm (4in) from the bottom. Screw the tap into the hole, fixing it behind with a large washer that will keep it watertight. Sit the water butt on bricks high enough to fit a watering can underneath. Finally, open the lid and direct any downpipes from guttering into the top of the wheelie bin, placing wire mesh over the opening to prevent leaves and other debris falling in. Leave the bin to fill with rain, closing the lid during dry periods.

Hacks 76–77
Wildlife-friendly watering can

Bees are a gardener's best friend and play an essential role in pollinating our plants. But you might be surprised to hear how many bees drown in the water left in the bottom of watering cans. Here are a few tricks to save the bees.

Bees will often fly into a watering can for a drink if it is left half-full of water. Unfortunately, they often fall into the water and drown. The most obvious way to stop this is never to leave any water in the can. You can tip leftover water back into a water butt, but you can't if you used a tap. It's a waste of water to pour it down the drain if your plants don't need it – and you don't want to over-water them.

My next hack is to push a plastic plant pot into the filling hole on top of the watering can. You might need to crush it slightly to squeeze it past the handle, but most small pots should fit perfectly into the hole. Ensure it fits snugly and there are no gaps around the edges. The drainage holes are usually too small for a bee to fly down, so it should keep them out. The pot will also prevent frogs from leaping into your watering can and drowning, too. You'll be surprised to discover that the pot can even remain in position when you're filling the can. It doesn't seem to slow the flow of water.

Leave a drink for the bees

During hot weather, bees can really struggle when there is a shortage of water, and many perish from thirst. I like to put a saucer of water over the watering can's filling hole after I've finished watering. I add small stones, ensuring they just protrude above the water's surface. This allows bees to land on the stones and drink without falling in and drowning in the saucer. The saucer also acts as another barrier to stop the bees from falling into the watering can.

Plug the gaps

Use any small plastic pot to prevent bees falling into the body of your watering can when it's not in use. Just fit it snugly over the main filling hole. To prevent bees from crawling down the nozzle and drowning, keep the rose in place. If you don't have a rose, you can simply stuff grass into the nozzle to block it up.

Hack 78
Hands-free watering

Going on holiday? Or just don't fancy having to water your plants too often? Here is a great way to automate your watering, so you don't have to worry about it. All you need is a bowl of water and some string.

This watering hack is quick and easy to set up. The theory is that damp string moves the moisture from the bowl of water to the compost in a plant pot slowly and gradually, using capillary action. Water will travel down the string from the source of water to the compost every time it dries out.

You will need
+ Bowl, bucket, or watering can
+ String
+ Scissors

More holiday watering hacks
+ Move plants in containers somewhere shady to reduce evaporation.
+ Place plants in containers on old damp towels, as roots can draw water upwards.
+ Give your plants a good watering before leaving home.

how to water hands-free

01 Fill a bowl, bucket, or watering can with water. Place it above the plants, perhaps on a table. This is really important as the method partly relies on gravity to get the water to the plants.

02 Cut lengths of string that will stretch from the water container to the plants in pots. You'll need one length for every pot. Soak the string in water to get the capillary action going.

03 Tie, or wrap round, one end of each string to a stone or weight. Put the stone in the watering can to keep the strings weighted down.

04 Run the other end of each string into a plant pot. Coil it on the compost for a few turns and push the tip a centimetre into the compost.

Hack 79
Cotton bud irrigation system

This is a great hack for watering plants while you are away, and it's very simple to put together.

This hack involves creating a self-watering, drip irrigation system using just one recycled plastic bottle and one cotton bud. Once you have set up your bottle and you are happy with the flow rate, place the dripping bottle on the surface of the compost next to the plant that needs watering while you're away. And then off you go on your holidays.

You will need

- Recycled plastic bottle (one litre size)
- Skewer or an incense stick
- Scissors or secateurs
- Cotton bud

Cover up

Mulching the surface of the soil with compost or rotted wood chips, ideally 5cm (2in) deep, will also help your plants survive when you are away. The mulch helps to retain moisture as well as suppress weeds, which compete with the plants for water. Pull out any surrounding weeds for this reason, too.

how to hack holiday watering

01 Make two holes in your water bottle, one in the centre of the lid and the other low down on the side. I use a lit incense stick to burn the two holes, or you can use a skewer.

02 Use scissors or secateurs to cut a cotton bud in half. Push the hollow end of each half into the two holes you've just made.

03 Take the lid off the bottle and fill it up with water. Put the lid back on and observe the speed at which water is dripping out of the cotton bud on the side of the bottle.

04 If you want the water to drip faster or slower, adjust the depth of the cotton bud in the lid. This alters the pressure in the bottle and the flow rate.

Hack 80
Milk bottle watering can

Plastic milk bottles have myriad uses in the garden. I like to make them into mini propagators (see p.22) or quick cloches (see p.23), as well as cut them up for plant labels (see p.28). They also make fantastic lightweight watering cans, perfect for sprinkling seedlings.

Rinse a plastic milk bottle thoroughly, then use a skewer (I actually use the tip of a biro) to puncture a few holes in the lid. Fill with water, put the lid on, and you've made yourself a watering can. The light spray through the holes in the lid simulates the effect of using a rose on the nozzle of your watering can, and is important to avoid damaging fragile seedlings. Squeeze the bottle to control the speed of the water flow.

Hack 81
Recycled bag watering

I love finding a use for old garden compost bags, which are tricky to recycle. They are stronger than most plastic sacks so perfect for holding enough water to keep a flowerbed happy while you are away.

Another hack I use to get more plants self-watered if I'm going away for a few days is to partly fill an old compost or builder's rubble bag with water. Tie a knot in the top of the bag so it is sealed and then make a tiny hole in the bottom of the bag with a pin. Place this bag on the surface of the compost. The water will slowly seep out of the bag over the course of a few days or a week and keep the compost nice and moist.

Mini version

For pots or hanging baskets you can do this with smaller bags, including ziplock freezer bags, plastic packaging, or even dog poo bags.

MAINTAIN

Hack 82
Grow dandelions

Many people see dandelions as purely weeds, and persecute them remorselessly when they appear in manicured lawns, but I would like to see more of them in our gardens. In fact, I would say plant more dandelions, don't pull them up!

I like to call them "nature's gold", not just because of their colour, but because of the richness they provide to both gardeners and wildlife. They are as beautiful as any sunflower with their bright golden flowerheads and attractive serrated foliage. Indeed in some countries, particularly in northern Europe and Scandinavia, going to see stunning meadows full of dandelions in spring is akin to the Japanese celebration of cherry blossom.

Wildlife loves dandelions, too. Leave a few in your garden to attract pollinating insects, which will turn their attention to pollinating your fruit trees and vegetables. The seeds and nectar from these "weeds" are an important source of food for birds, butterflies, bees, beetles, and other insects, while rabbits adore the nutritious leaves.

Dandelion benefits

- Their roots can be made into coffee or root beer.
- The leaves can be used as an alternative to salad leaves.
- Dandelion flowers can be made into delicious tea, wine, or cordial.

Plant dandelions in a raised bed

Dig up one or two dandelions and chop the thick taproot into 2cm (¾in) lengths. Plant each section of root into the compost in your raised bed, 2cm (¾in) deep and 15cm (6in) apart. Each section of root will grow and attract pollinators, as well as rewarding you with gorgeous yellow blooms in spring.

Hack 83
Aerate your lawn

A lush green lawn looks lovely, but if it gets a lot of use the soil below will quickly become compacted. This results in brown, dying grass, because the roots get crushed, can't spread out, and can't absorb water and nutrients.

However, the compaction of the lawn in a small garden can easily be resolved by using a garden fork. Push the fork into the ground so the tines are about 10cm (4in) below the surface and give it a little wiggle (or heave) on the handle. Repeat this all over your lawn at a spacing of about every 15cm (6in). Not only is it a good workout for your muscles, but your lawn will quickly recover and return to its natural green colour. For larger lawns you can hire machines called aerators which will do a similar job, on a much larger scale.

Spiky shoes

It is possible to purchase or rent a pair of shoes with lots of large spikes on the soles. These are specifically designed to create holes in the lawn and break up any compaction. Nothing could be simpler than aerating the lawn while you walk around the garden with a cup of coffee in your hand.

MAINTAIN

Hack 84
Spoon water diffuser

Gardeners often attach a rose to a watering can to change the flow of water into a lighter drizzle or spray. If you don't have a rose, try this hack.

Attach a dessert spoon to the end of the can's nozzle using hose clips (jubilee clips) or cable ties so that the bowl of the spoon sits just below where the water tips out. The water from the watering can sloshes onto the spoon and bounces off it, distributing the water over a wider area than if you were just pouring it through the nozzle.

When to water?

The most effective time is early in the morning, so the plant can soak up moisture before it gets too hot. Evening is the second-best time, but it can attract slugs and leave soil soggy overnight, which might cause some plants to rot. Watering during the middle of the day can lead to water evaporating before it soaks into the ground and finds plant roots.

Hack 85
Chelsea chop

If you enjoyed a wonderful splash of colour from your herbaceous perennials in late spring, chances are you can enjoy it again later in the year if you give your plants the "Chelsea chop".

It's called the "Chelsea chop" because gardeners tend to do this around the time of the Royal Horticultural Society Chelsea Flower Show. Use hand shears or secateurs to chop back about two-thirds of the new growth in late spring. This will encourage more growth later on in the season, giving you a double flush of flowers throughout the year. If you do this to half your plants, it will also give you a better depth to your flower border, as you'll have the same plant but at two different stages in their growth and height.

Remember also to keep deadheading repeat-flowering plants such as roses, geraniums, and dahlias (see p.140).

MAINTAIN

Hack 86
Secateur savvy

There are two different types of secateurs used in the garden: bypass and anvil. Bypass versions will give you much better results when pruning, so read on for my guide to how to use them correctly.

Anvil secateurs use a crushing action to make their cut, with one blade coming directly down on top of another one, and for this reason are not considered great for pruning because it damages the plant's stem.

Bypass secateurs are much better (and usually more expensive). They use a motion like a pair of scissors, with one blade cutting across another fixed "jaw" or "beak". This produces a much cleaner cut, with less chance of infection or damaging plant tissues. The stem will heal much faster from a bypass cut.

Many gardeners don't realize that there is a correct way to use bypass secateurs. When cutting a stem or branch, the sharp, moving blade side of the secateurs should be facing the section of the plant you wish to retain. The fixed blade should face away from it, towards the section you are going to remove. The design of bypass secateurs means that the moving blade can be placed right next to where you wish to cut. The fixed blade has a small gap, so can't be placed flush to where you want to cut, which can result in crushing and therefore damaging the tip of the stem that you wished to keep. This can result in the stem dying back and infecting the plant.

Hack 87
Deadhead for more flowers

If you'd like your plants to produce flowers for longer, deadheading them is the answer. Deadheading means removing the flowerheads once they have just started to go over, and before they turn to seed.

Deadheading usually results in a second flush of flowering, as well as making the plant look tidier. The theory is that when you remove a flower, it stops it producing seeds, and so the plant will channel its energy into forming more flowers, with the intention of these new ones producing seeds instead. Deadheading triggers a plant's innate sense of reproduction and survival of its species.

There are various ways of deadheading a plant. With roses I tend to use my finger and thumb to snap the flowerhead off just below it. However, you can also cut back to the first set of five leaves below the flowerhead with a pair of secateurs. Plants with large flowering stems, such as lupin and penstemon, need the entire flower spike removed, while some bedding plants can have their flowers pulled off by hand as they start to go over.

Bedding plants and annuals, including petunias, geraniums, and marigolds, are popular candidates for deadheading to prolong their flowering period. Most herbaceous perennials will also produce more flowers if their spent flowerheads are removed. These can include penstemons, dahlias, daffodils, delphiniums, and lupins. Many shrubs also benefit from some deadheading, including roses, spirea, hebe, weigela, and tree peonies.

Keep the garden tidy

Deadheading prevents prolific self-seeders such as *Verbena bonariensis*, *Nigella* (Love-in-a-Mist), borage, and even dandelions from spreading their seeds everywhere. Improving the appearance of plants is another reason for deadheading. I sometimes deadhead camellias and rhododendrons to improve their appearance. Don't be overzealous when removing spent flowerheads – leave some to produce seedheads to sustain wildlife over winter.

Hack 88
No-fuss rose pruning

I often see gardeners going to great lengths to explain the intricacies of pruning roses, giving precise details of the angle at which a pruning cut should be made, and to exactly how many millimetres a shoot should be cut.

However, I've found that with many of the roses I've got growing in my garden, none of this fussing about makes much difference. If you are a bit impatient like me, and like getting jobs done quickly and with minimal faff, then give my method a try.

To tidy up a rose bush, simply take out a hedge cutter and cut all the growth back by about two-thirds. It's very quick to do with a hedge trimmer. In my experience, rose bushes will bounce back quickly the following year and still produce just as many flowers as if you'd done it methodically and carefully as it is traditionally taught.

MAINTAIN

Hack 89
Anti-sting sock gauntlets

When you are gardening you might occasionally get stung on your arms by nettles, or certain plants may give you a rash. For example, some people's skin reacts to hairy plants such as courgettes, echiums, or borage.

My simple hack to avoid this is to take an old pair of long socks, the thicker the better, and cut the toes off. Then simply slide them over your hands and up onto your forearms. You now have a set of free gauntlets to protect your arms and keep you sting-free while you weed.

Hack 90
Grow tomatoes up strings

Tomatoes always need some support, or their weight will make them flop over. I find it is much easier to train them up strings rather than having to insert canes to keep each individual tomato plant upright.

My way of growing tomatoes is this. I create a tripod of three canes, tied at the top, at both ends of a row, then I tie another cane stretching from one tripod to the other to create a cross-bar.

I then "plant" lengths of string, followed by tomatoes, into the soil, burying the string below each seedling's root ball. I then tie the string to the cross-bar above the plant. Hopefully this method will provide you with huge gluts of delicious tomatoes.

Hand saver

One of the side effects of gardening is dirty fingernails. My hack for keeping them clean is to scratch them into a bar of soap before you start gardening. The soap under your nails acts as a barrier and prevents the dirt from collecting there. Once you've finished gardening, run your fingers under the tap and the soap (and any excess dirt) washes away.

how to grow happy tomatoes

01 Position lengths of string at regular intervals where you plan to add your tomatoes. Make sure the string will reach your cross-bar.

02 I plant my tomato seedlings 35cm (14in) apart into the soil, next to a string, then tie the loose end of the string to the cane cross-bar.

03 Twist each tomato around its vertical string and watch them as they continue to grow, tying them to the string as necessary.

Hacks 91–94
Recycle your tights

If you have a pair of old tights somewhere in the house, instead of chucking them in the bin, here are my handy hacks for recycling them in the garden.

I suspect that plenty of gardeners wear tights under their trousers to provide an extra layer of warmth during the colder months. Once they have reached the end of their life as clothing tights can be reused. They make an excellent nylon "rope" that can be used as a tree tie, and are strong enough to use as pot liners, or a handy pot storage feature.

Flexible tree ties

Tights make excellent tree ties as they are nice and flexible, so the material stretches as the tree grows without cutting into the bark. If you make a big, thick knot between the tree and the stake, the soft tights will protect the tree from damaging itself if the wind blows the tree onto the stake.

Compost saver

Cut old tights into small sections and put them at the bottom of pots. The tights prevent compost from washing out of the drainage holes in the bottom, yet are porous enough for excess liquid to drain away easily. If you don't have any tights, you can use paper coffee filters instead.

Don't forget your bra

You can also recycle an old bra. The cups can be filled with compost and trailing plants such as geraniums or even strawberries. I also like to use bras as melon supports in the greenhouse. The flexible yet strong material means it can prevent heavy fruit from dropping off the vine and falling on the ground. Warning: if there is a bra in the house, but it doesn't actually belong to you, I strongly recommend you ask the owner first. I got into terrible trouble once for using a bra as a melon support without permission.

MAINTAIN

Pot storage

Hang a pair of tights from a nail in the potting shed and stack all your smaller pots into the legs. Use scissors to cut a hole in the toe end. You now have a pot dispenser. Whenever you need a pot, simply pull one from the toe and the rest will stay inside the nylons.

Hack 95
Use a clove hitch

Learning how to tie knots can be helpful in the garden. The one I use most is the clove hitch. It's a very easy knot to tie, and is simple to adjust. It is the essential knot for any budding gardener.

I use a clove hitch for tying plant supports such as wigwams together, to create a tight line for erecting a fence, or for marking out a border for edging. You can also use it for tying plants to upright supports, and even for tying tools up for storage. It's a good knot for tying to cylindrical objects such as a branch. Clove hitches are also easy to make adjustments such as tightening or loosening, or for moving along a branch.

How to tie a clove hitch

+ Wrap your string or rope around a branch and cross the string over.
+ Wrap the string around again, crossing over in the other direction. If the first time you wrapped over you ended up on the right side, the second wrap should cross over the left, and vice versa.
+ Bring it around again, but this time push the end of the string under between the first two wraps. You now have a clove hitch.

Hack 96
Handy string saver

Here is a quick hack to prevent balls of string or twine becoming tangled once you've started using them.

After making your dispenser, simply pull out the string or twine to the desired length whenever you need it. I always keep a pair of scissors with the string in the upturned bottle for convenience.

how to make a string dispenser

01 Use a skewer or a small screw to create a hole in the centre of the lid of a large recycled plastic bottle.

02 Use a pair of scissors or knife to carefully cut off the lower half of the plastic bottle.

03 Screw the top half of the bottle to the wall of your shed, with the lid facing downwards.

04 Remove the lid and put your ball of string in the bottle. Pull the string through the opening. Thread about 10cm (4in) of string though the hole in the lid, then screw the lid back on.

Hack 97
Terracotta pot watering

In central and southern America, gardeners fill a type of terracotta pot with water and bury it in the ground next to their plants to keep them well watered. It is called an *olla* (which means "an earthen pot used for holding water" in Spanish).

This hack emulates an *olla* and is handy for watering plants if you're going away, or too busy to water. Make sure the pot you choose isn't glazed or painted, which can prevent the water from seeping out. Unglazed clay is naturally porous and allows water to seep out of the pot gradually and into the surrounding soil. This in turn waters the nearby plants and nourishes the roots. Due to capillary action, the water only moves out of the pot when the surrounding soil is lacking in moisture.

how to bury an *olla*

01 Seal the drainage hole of a terracotta pot with reusable adhesive such as blu tack – or shove a wine cork into it.

02 Bury the pot in the soil or compost next to a plant that needs watering, being careful not to damage the roots.

03 Ensure just the lip or top 1–2cm (½–¾in) of the pot protrudes above the surface.

04 Fill the pot with water and place a lid (I use a saucer) on top to prevent evaporation.

Hack 98
Pea sticks from prunings

If you're lucky enough to have a garden large enough for a few trees and shrubs, then you'll probably discover that you often need to give them a prune to keep them healthy and tidy. Don't discard your twiggy prunings – they can make supports for your pea plants.

Pea plants grow to about 1m (3ft) high, and because they are climbers they need something to scramble up. Most gardeners use nets stretched between two upright posts for the peas to climb up. However, I prefer to recycle my prunings as it is easy, free, and sustainable. It also looks much prettier in a kitchen garden. I find the best shrubs for this are hazel or lime because they have a lovely zigzag shape, but most twiggy branches will do.

Select twiggy branches that are about 1m (3ft) long and push them into the ground next to each spot where you have either planted or sown a row of peas. The peas will quickly grab onto the branches and scramble up with their tendrils. Once you've finished harvesting peas, you can add the sticks to your compost.

Hack 99
Use a colour wheel

Garden designers often use a colour wheel (you can find one online) to create the desired effect or ambience. If you place two plants in shades from opposite sides of the wheel next to each other in a border or container, you'll get the most vivid contrast.

As a very general rule, hot colours such as reds, oranges, and yellows create an atmosphere of vibrancy and excitement, while softer pastel colours such as pale blue, cream, and mauve create a sense of tranquillity and serenity.

If you mix colours up when designing a flower border you can create some striking combinations, using either harmonious or striking contrasts. My favourite colour contrast is orange or yellow juxtaposed with blues and purples, such as *Achillea* 'Golden Plate' with blue salvias or nepeta. If you place neighbours on the colour wheel near each other in a flowerbed you can create a more harmonious feel, although if the colours are too close you can end up with a clash.

Hack 100
Shape your lawn

If you want to create a flowerbed with a curved edge, dig a circular plot for a new tree, or simply define a new boundary for your lawn, try this hack.

It can be tricky to mark out the curved edge of a lawn or flowerbed when you're creating one from scratch. I like to lay an old plastic hose on the ground to create my shapes and contours. It is light and easy to move, allowing you to play around with different ideas. Once you've marked your desired shape with the hose, cut it out with a spade or half-moon tool.

Warm it up

Your hose is far more pliable if you leave it in the sun to warm up first. On colder days, run some hot water through it to soften the plastic.

DESIGN

Hack 101
Wheelbarrow chair

Enjoyable as gardening is, we all need a sit down occasionally to take the weight off and regain some energy for the next task. This hack is an instant fix.

The quickest way to make a garden seat is to upturn your wheelbarrow (so the handles are resting on the ground) and lean it against a tree or wall. A wheelbarrow makes a surprisingly comfortable seat, particularly if you place cushions and blankets in it. Its interior has a natural recline which is at the perfect angle for sitting in. If you're careful when you sit down, you don't even need to lean the barrow on anything, as your weight counterbalances it from falling over.

Hack 102
Make a dead hedge

Is there a messy area in your garden that you're not particularly proud of and would rather others didn't see? For me, it is my compost area, where I leave piles of clippings, prunings, pots, labels, and buckets of liquid nettle fertilizer until I'm ready to sort them out.

Creating a dead hedge is an easy, and free, way of screening an unsightly area or creating privacy in your garden. Not only should a dead hedge not cost you a penny, but unlike living hedges, you don't need to trim it to keep it in shape. And it's a great way of using up woody prunings and clippings. I've got some living hedges in part of my garden, so I always add the clippings from that to my dead hedge. Best of all, a dead hedge should attract lots of wildlife to your garden.

Decide where you wish to create the dead hedge and push posts into the ground at 50cm (20in) intervals along its length. Add a parallel set of posts about 40cm (16in) away. Collect woody prunings and garden debris and push them into the gap between the two rows of posts. Firm and push down material as you add it, to make the hedge as dense as possible. Continue building up your dead hedge until you reach the top of the posts. As the material rots down over time, add more twiggy or woody material.

Hack 103
Three sisters

This is an ingenious method of growing three different plants harmoniously in the same bed. It was devised by Native Americans and it's really useful if you are short of space in the garden.

The three sisters (or crops) are sweetcorn, climbing beans, and pumpkins or squashes. All three plants grow in harmony and provide a benefit to each other. The climbing beans fix nitrogen in the soil, which feeds the sweetcorn and the squash. The upright stems of the sweetcorn provide a climbing structure for the beans to scramble up. And the squashes sprawl along the ground, shading the base of the other crops, helping to suppress competing weeds, retaining moisture, and reducing evaporation.

DESIGN

Hack 104
Plant a pumpkin right way round

Pumpkins and squashes know exactly which direction they intend to grow in as soon as they are in the ground. This hack is really worth knowing, as it can be very tricky to change their direction once they've got going.

Look for your seedling's first true leaf. The plant will nearly always grow in the opposite direction to that leaf. So if you intend to train your plant to trail across a bed, or up a trellis or wigwam, point the first leaf away from the structure, and the remainder of the growth will grow where you intend.

Hack 105
Toilet roll bird feeder

One of the many benefits of having a garden is watching the wonderful wildlife that become regular visitors to your plants. However, sometimes our feathered friends can be shy and need encouragement.

This easy hack should have birds flocking to your garden in no time. You can make a very easy bird feeder with just a toilet roll tube and a few simple ingredients. Make as many as you like and hang them from a branch of a tree, then sit back and enjoy watching all the birds visit your feeders.

You will need

+ Toilet roll tube
+ String
+ Peanut butter
+ Knife
+ Bird seed
+ Small tray

how to make a treat for the birds

01 Thread string through your toilet roll tube. Cut the string long enough to hang from your chosen spot.

02 Use a kitchen knife to spread peanut butter all over the tube. Make sure there are no gaps..

03 Pour bird seed into a small clean tray and roll your tube in it so the seeds stick to the peanut butter and the tube is completely covered.

04 Hang your bird feeder in a suitable spot.

Hack 106
Parasol grapevine trainer

Instead of throwing away an old garden or beach parasol, you can grow climbers up it. I grow a grapevine up mine, but this hack works with any type of climbing plant.

First remove all the cloth sections from your parasol. Dig a hole where you want your climber to grow and push in the base of the parasol. Fill the hole with the displaced soil or, if you want to make it more secure, add rubble to the hole or set the base in concrete.

Once the parasol is firmly positioned, open it up to expose its umbrella-shaped structure. Plant a wine grapevine at the base. As it grows, train the shoots to follow the "ribs" of the parasol and after two or three years you will have a leafy canopy to sit under.

Grow annuals as well

Annuals such as climbing beans, runner beans, and sweet peas are usually grown up a wigwam of bamboo canes or hazel sticks, but you can try this instead with your recycled parasol. Attach strings to the canopy structure, equally spaced about 20cm (8in) apart. Tie the end of each string to a tent peg pushed into the ground below. Plant your annuals at the base of each string and they will climb up to the top.

Hack 107
Simple pallet raised bed

This is probably the easiest way to make a raised bed that you will ever encounter. It's almost instant and requires next to no DIY skills. All you need is one recycled pallet (p.51).

Lay the pallet on the ground where you want your raised bed to be. It's best to do this on grass or soil rather than a patio or tarmac, as this raised bed won't be very deep, so the roots of the plants need to grow into the soil below. If laying on a lawn, you don't need to remove the turf first; it won't grow through the pallet once filled with soil.

Prise the slats from the top of the pallet using a crowbar. Nail or screw four of them to the sides, making a shallow open box. Fill the raised bed with garden compost. Use your hands to push the compost right into all the corners, and fill the bed to just below the top. You're now ready to put plants into the soil. Three of the best for a pallet raised bed are strawberries, herbs, and salad leaves.

You will need
+ One pallet
+ Crowbar
+ Hammer and nails or screwdriver and screws
+ Compost
+ Plants

Hack 108
Hosepipe raised bed

Most raised beds are made from wood or bricks, but you can make one out of almost anything. If you have an old hosepipe lying around, use it to create the sides of a small circular raised bed.

To create the circle shape for the raised bed, tie the ends of a 50cm (20in) piece of string to two bamboo canes. Push one cane into the ground where you would like the centre of your bed to be. Pull the string taut and then walk in a circle using the end of the other bamboo cane to scratch out the edge of the bed.

Cut some wood stakes (I used six branches from my hazel tree as stakes). Push them into the ground at 25cm (10in) intervals on the outline of the 1m- (3ft-) wide circle you marked. Wrap or weave your hose around the stakes, building height until you have created your circular bed. Use a pair of loppers to trim your stakes so that they are flush with or sit just above your raised bed. This will make it look neater.

Self-watering feature

If there is a length of hose left over after making the bed, you can add a self-watering feature. Use a skewer or knife to carefully create some holes in the side of the raised bed. Attach the free end of the hose to your outside tap or water butt and turn it on. Your raised bed will now water the plants by dripping from its leaky hose. If you attach this to a timer on your outside tap, it you can go on holiday and your raised bed will water itself.

DESIGN

Hack 109
Shoe rack herb garden

Reckon you don't have enough space for a herb garden? Then think again. With a cheap, space-saving shoe storage rack, which you can hang on the back of a door, you can create a vertical herb garden either indoors or on your shed.

Most shoe holders have 12 or 16 pockets, depending on their configuration. Slot a range of different herbs in small pots into each of the pockets. You can hang the shoe storage rack on the back of a shed door or, if you don't have a shed, hang them on a curtain rail in the house or from your kitchen door. If you do the latter, if couldn't be easier to pick a sprig to flavour your dishes as you cook.

I've found that herbs such as coriander, chervil, parsley, tarragon, basil, thyme, and marjoram thrive in these shoe-storage pockets. Avoid slightly larger, shrubby herbs such as rosemary and sage unless you only intend to keep them in the planter for a few weeks, before they outgrow their space. I've found that mint works to an extent, but you have to keep it well watered as mint doesn't like to dry out.

Hack 110
Croc containers

Growing plants in old shoes or boots is a wonderful way of repurposing something that might otherwise be thrown away. Some shoes have beautiful shapes and make a great feature when plants are thriving in them.

You could try trailing plants such as geraniums, nasturtiums, strawberries, or even have tumbling tomatoes spilling out of the top of a tall wellington boot. Perhaps plant some succulents such as echeverias and sempervirens in an old croc-style shoe. Don't forget to make a hole in or two the bottom of a wellington boot to allow excess moisture to drain away. Crocs don't need extra drainage, as they already have plenty of gaps for water to escape through.

Place the boots or shoes by your back door or somewhere else prominent to make an attractive display. You can hang crocs up by old shoelaces from your fence or garden wall too. Literally gardening on a shoestring!

Hack 111
Mini terrarium

In recent years terrariums have had a huge revival. You can buy beautiful versions, but if you want to give it a try for free, then have a go creating a terrarium in a glass jar. My only purchase was some activated charcoal.

In the supermarket you'll notice many pickles, chocolate or hazelnut spreads, and jams are sold in surprisingly ornate or bell-shaped jars. They make a beautiful terrarium when filled with a small fern or other plant. Have a look in your garden or local park for a tiny piece of rotting wood or stick that will fit in the jar. You might find some moss on your patio or roof, soil in your flowerbed, and gravel from your drive. I found a tiny free fern growing in a crack in my garden wall. Keep your terrarium somewhere light and cool indoors, but out of direct sunlight.

how to make a jam jar terrarium

01 Clean your jar, remove its labels, and leave it to dry. Place a layer of gravel on the upturned lid, then add a layer of soil or garden compost, and moss, if you like.

02 Sprinkle a pinch of activated charcoal on top. This helps filter toxins to keep the air and water pure, as well as preventing mould and bacteria building up.

03 Position your tiny, rotted piece of timber and finally plant your fern. Spray the foliage with water to revitalize it, and then place the jar over the whole display and screw it to the lid.

04 The fern will release moisture, which will condense and run back into the soil, keeping the fern alive. If your fern does look as if it is drying out, give it an occasional mist of water.

Hack 112
Quick stick seat

Here is another quick and easy way to create a seat, this time using just three sticks and a blanket.

You will need
+ Three sturdy sticks
+ String
+ Blanket or sheet
+ Rope

how to create a stick seat

01 Grab two sturdy sticks and tie them together at the top with string. Lean them against a wall or tree and splay the sticks so they feel sturdy.

02 Fold a blanket, sheet, or tarpaulin in half and tie all four corners together, with rope, leaving a long end.

DESIGN

03 Use the long end to attach this knot to where the two sticks meet at the top.

04 Take your third stick and slide it into the fold at the bottom of the blanket.

05 Rest the stick on the two uprights. You now have a comfortable seat to relax in while watching the world or wildlife go by.

Hack 113
Keyhole gardening

A keyhole garden is a round raised bed for growing edibles in, with a compost heap in the centre. It is the ultimate sustainable method of growing food, reducing the need to water and feed your plants.

From above, the bed has the shape of a keyhole, with a notch in the circle providing access to the compost heap. Keyhole gardening originated in Lesotho, southern Africa, for growing food in impoverished soil and dry conditions. The compost leaches into the surrounding soil, feeding plants, so the compost container in the centre needs to be made from permeable material. I usually use chicken wire. Feed the compost heap with your garden and kitchen waste and it will break down and enrich the nearby soil, adding nutrients and improving the soil structure. Not only does this reduce the need for feeding the plants, but it also reduces the need for watering, as the surrounding compost has better moisture-retaining qualities.

When adding soil to the raised bed, try to slope the surface so that it is higher around the compost bin and lower around the edges. Gravity should help the nutrients from the compost to move slowly outwards to reach all of the keyhole bed.

DESIGN

Hack 114
Edimental plants

Not all of us have room in the garden to grow both food crops and pretty ornamental plants. If you don't have room for both types, you could try "edimental" plants – with both ornamental and edible qualities.

You can combine these plants for a truly delectable and delicious look and taste. The French have been doing it for centuries in their kitchen gardens or "potagers", so called because ingredients grown there could be made into a soup or potage. They quickly discovered that a functional garden growing for the kitchen can also look beautiful.

You can do something similar. Think of the brightly coloured stems of chard, the purple leaves from a pink elderflower bush, or the architectural flowerheads of angelica or fennel in your flower border. The only restriction to combining edible and ornamental plants is your creative and artistic imagination. You'd be amazed at how many there are. Here are my five favourites.

Dahlias

Dahlias produce beautiful flowers, but did you know that they were introduced to Europe as an edible crop? It was thought that the tubers (swollen roots) would make a great alternative to potatoes. Next time you dig them up to store over winter, try pulling off a few tubers and boiling, roasting, or frying them. My favourite is dahlia chips (see also p.76).

Bistort

This gorgeous pink-, white-, or red-flowered herbaceous plant is often seen in flower borders. It's a magnet for bees as well as being a feast for the eyes – and you can eat the leaves either fresh or cooked. It's a great spinach substitute.

Nasturtiums

These popular annuals come in hot colours such as red, orange, and yellow. The flowers have a unique, peppery flavour. But my favourite way to eat them is to harvest the seeds. They have a nutty, yet quite spicy, taste. In fact, they are quite hot! You can also pickle them in vinegar and use them as an alternative to pickled capers.

Hemerocallis

Also known as the day lily, the flowers of this perennial appear for just one day. But don't worry, it produces lots more! Almost all parts of the plant can be eaten, including the petals, roots, leaves, and flower buds. Please note, some "true" lilies are poisonous, so don't confuse the two.

Chives

Many of us grow these herbs for their mildly onion-flavoured hollow stems, but they also produce beautiful blue flowers. Grow them at the front of a flower border for a pretty, yet edible, display.

Index

air circulation 32
alliums 81
annuals, training 170
anti-sting sock gauntlets 143
aphids 64
ash 12, 95

back savers 13
bags, recycled bag watering 130
bananas: banana skin plant food 104–105
　ripening tomatoes with 104
beans 166
beds and borders: hosepipe raised bed 172
　mulching borders 112
　no-dig beds 116–17
　simple pallet raised bed 171
bee-friendly watering can 122–23
beer traps 63
bindweed liquid feed 108–109
birds: bird feeders 75, 168–69
　decoy strawberries 74
　feather and potato bird scarer 66–69
　spicy bird seed 75
bistort 186
blackfly 65
bras 148
brassicas 71
bulbs, container bulb saver 78–79

cabbage white butterflies 81
cabbages 81
cacti, growing from dragon fruit 44–45
cardboard seed pots 10–11
carrot root fly 81
carrots: companion planting 81
　growing carrots for flowers 46–47
catmint 80
chairs: quick stick seat 180–81
　wheelbarrow chairs 163
cheese boxes, storing seeds in 18–19
Chelsea chop 136–37
chives 187
climbing plants, training 41, 170
cloches, milk carton 23
clove hitches 150–51
coat hanger hoe 118–19
coffee booster 106
colour wheels 160–61
comfrey feed 86–87, 89
companion planting 81
compost: acid effect 98
　chopping your compost 99
　compost saver 148
　leaf mould 92–93
　mole hill compost 94
　rotating 103
　slow-cooking compost 97
　space-saving composting 96–97
　two-bucket wormery 90–91
　watering 102
　what to compost 96, 102
　wood ash compost booster 95
compost bins: compost bin rat repeller 98
　dead hedges 164–65
　keyhole gardening 182–83
　recycled pallet compost bay 100–101
containers see pots
copper slug repellents 63
cork plant labels 29

cotton bud irrigation system 126–27
croc containers 176–77
crop rotation 71
cutlery plant labels 29
cuttings: hardwood rose cuttings 38–39
　lavender cuttings 34
　sweet pea tip cuttings 35

dahlia tubers 76, 185
dandelions 131
dead hedges 164–65
deadheading 140–41
dibbers, fork handle 54
digging, no-dig gardening 114–17
diseases: companion planting 81
　crop rotation 71
　mildew spray 70
disposable cutlery plant labels 29
dragon fruit, growing a cactus from 44–45

earwig catchers, flowerpot 76–77
edimental plants 184–87
eggshell fertilizer 107
eye protectors, spice jar 72–73

feather and potato bird scarer 66–69
feeds and fertilizers: banana skin plant food 104–05
　bindweed liquid feed 108–109
　coffee booster 106
　eggshell fertilizer 107
　liquid plant food 86–89
　wood ash 95
fingernails, dirty 144
flowers: deadheading 140–41

INDEX

growing carrots for flowers 46–47
fork handle dibbers 54
fruit: growing a cactus from a dragon fruit 44–45
white pebbles for ripening 42–43

grapevine trainers, parasol 170
greenhouses, storage box 32–33
gutters, growing early peas in 41

hand tools, storing in sand 56–57
hedgehog homes 60
hedges, dead 164–65
heliotropism 31
hemerocallis 187
herb gardens, shoe rack 174–75
hoe, coat hanger 118–19
holiday watering hacks 124, 126–27, 130, 172
horsetail 116
hoses 162
 hose and rake seed driller 48–49
 hosepipe raised bed 172
houseplants, feeding 107

irrigation systems: cotton bud irrigation system 126–27
 hands-free watering 124–25

jam jar terrarium 178–79
Japanese knotweed 116

keyhole gardening 182–83
knots, clove hitches 150–51

labels: free plant labels 26–29
 labelling seed boxes 18–19
ladybird hotels 64
lavender cuttings 34
lawns: aerating 132–33
 perfecting lawn edges 113
 shaping 162
leaves: leaf mould 92–93

mowing 93
picking up 93
pricking out seedlings 12
legumes 71
long-handled tools 13

marigolds 81
melon supports 148
mesh potato tower 52–53
mildew, milk spray 70
milk cartons: milk bottle watering can 128–29
 milk carton cloche 23
 milk carton propagator 22
 plant labels 28
mole hills 94
mulching 112, 126

nasturtiums 81, 186
nettles: anti-sting sock gauntlets 143
 nettle feed 86–87, 88–89
newspaper seed pots 10
no-dig gardening 114–17

olla 154–55
ornamental plants 185–87

pallets 51
 pallet seed trays 15
 pallet tool unit 51
 recycled pallet compost bay 100–101
 simple pallet raised bed 171
 vertical strawberry planter 40
parasol grapevine trainer 170
patios, de-weeding 82–83
peas: climbing frames 41
 growing early peas in gutters 41
 pea shoots 41
 pea sticks 156–57
pebbles: plant labels 28
 white pebbles for ripening fruit 42–43
peg plant labels 29

pests: companion planting 81
 crop rotation 71
 see also individual pests
planks 62
plant food *see* feeds and fertilizer
planters, vertical strawberry 40
planting: companion planting 81
 planting sunflowers facing east 31
 using a pot to make a planting hole 30
pollen-rich plants 64
potash 95
potassium 95
potatoes 71
 feather and potato bird scarer 66–69
 mesh potato tower 52–53
pots: cardboard seed pots 10–11
 container bulb saver 78–79
 croc containers 176–77
 flowerpot earwig catchers 76–77
 growing early peas in gutters 41
 pot storage 149
 recycled bag watering 130
 terracotta pot watering 154–55
 using a pot to make a planting hole 30
 vertical strawberry planter 40
propagation: cutting edge trick 36
 milk carton propagator 22
 rosemary propagation 36–37
pruning: Chelsea chop 136–37
 no-fuss rose pruning 142
 pea sticks from prunings 156–57
pumpkins 166, 167

rainwater, collecting 120–21
raised beds: hosepipe raised bed 172
 keyhole gardening 182–83
 simple pallet raised bed 171
rake head storage 55
rat-proof compost bins 98

ripening fruit, white pebbles for 42–43
root vegetables 71
rosemary propagation 36–37
roses: hardwood rose cuttings 38–39
no-fuss rose pruning 142

salt, banishing slugs with 61
sand: mixing small seeds with 12
storing hand tools in sand 56–57
seats: quick stick seat 180–81
wheelbarrow chair 163
secateurs, types of 139
seed driller, hose and rake 48–49
seed trays, pallet 15
seedlings: milk carton cloche 23
pricking out 12
seeds: cardboard seed pots 10–11
collecting seeds for free 16–17
DIY seed envelopes 20–21
mixing small seeds with sand 12
sowing large seeds on their side 14
sowing standing up 13
storing in cheese boxes 18–19
toilet roll planters 24–25
sheep's wool slug repellent 62
shoes: croc containers 176–77
shoe rack herb garden 174–75
spiky shoes 132
slugs and snails 60–63, 135
sock gauntlets, anti-sting 143
soil, adding organic matter to 96
sowing seeds: cardboard seed pots 10–11
hose and rake seed driller 48–49
milk carton propagator 22
mixing small seeds with sand 12
pallet seed trays 15
sowing large seeds on their side 14
sowing standing up 13
toilet roll planters 24–25

spice jar eye protectors 72–73
spicy bird seed 75
spiky shoes 132
spoon water diffuser 134–35
squashes 166
squirrels 75
container bulb saver 78–79
sticks: pea sticks from prunings 156–57
plant labels 28
quick stick seat 180–81
stick trug 50
sticky tape blackfly traps 65
storage: pot storage 149
rake head storage 55
storing hand tools in sand 56–57
storing seeds 18–21
storage box mini greenhouses 32–33
strawberries 148
decoy strawberries 74
vertical strawberry planter 40
string: growing tomatoes up strings 144–45
handy string dispenser 152–53
sunflowers, plant facing east 31
sweet pea tip cuttings 35
sweetcorn 166

terracotta pot watering 154–55
terrarium, jam jar 178–79
three sisters 166
tights, recycling 146–49
toilet rolls: toilet roll bird feeder 168–69
toilet roll planters 24–25
tomatoes: companion planting 81
growing up strings 144–45
ripening 104
tools: coat hanger hoe 118–19
fork handle dibbers 54
long-handled tools 13
pallet tool unit 51
rake head storage 55

secateurs 139
storing hand tools in sand 56–57
trainers, parasol grapevine 170
tree ties, flexible 146–47
trugs, stick 50
two-bucket wormery 90–91

vegetables: crop rotation 71
sowing large seeds on their side 14
three sisters 166
vertical growing: shoe rack herb garden 174–75
vertical strawberry planter 40

watering: collecting rainwater 120–21
cotton bud irrigation system 126–27
hands-free watering 124–25
recycled bag watering 130
self-watering beds 172
terracotta pot watering 154–55
watering compost 102
when to water 135
watering cans: milk bottles 128–29
spoon water diffuser 134–35
wildlife-friendly 122–23
weeds: de-weeding your patio 82–83
eradicating invasive weeds 116
mulching 112
wheelbarrow chair 163
wheelie bins, collecting rainwater in 121
whitefly 81
wildlife: benefits of dandelions 131
wildlife-friendly watering cans 122–23
wine cork plant labels 29
wood ash 95
wormeries, two-bucket 90–91

Acknowledgements

I would love to thank the wonderful team at DK for all their support throughout *Way to Grow*'s journey from concept to publication. I'd particularly like to thank Ruth O'Rourke for all her guidance and support and for believing in the idea right from the start. And to Alastair Laing and Barbara Zuniga for their project management and editing skills and turning up for all those photo shoots, no matter what the weather. Also, I owe a huge debt of gratitude to Hayley Reed and Silvia Dembner for their fantastic marketing and publicity campaigns and great advice. Massive thanks also to Jason Ingram for his superb photography and for his patience while we tried to set up the shots. Thank you too to Clare Double for editing my words and for her ability to rewrite my waffly sentences into something coherent that sounds good. Finally, huge thank you to my agent Jo Cantello from Wolfsong Media for all her help and encouragement with making *Way to Grow* happen.

Picture credits

The publisher would like to thank the following for their kind permission to reproduce their photographs:

(Key: a-above; b-below/bottom; c-centre; f-far; l-left; r-right; t-top)

123RF.com: asphoto777 165; **Alamy Stock Photo**: Holmes Garden Photos / Neil Holmes 137, Michelle Carden Photography 115, Purple Marbles Garden 16; **Dreamstime.com**: Trevor Allen 187b, Yulia Babkina 157, Tatiana Belova 186tl, Allison Carmody 187cl, Keldridge82 64, Lenatru 186b, Ihar Mamchyts 184; **Shutterstock.com**: Holly S Cannon 161

Senior Editor Alastair Laing
Gardening Design Manager Barbara Zuniga
Senior Production Editor Tony Phipps
Senior Production Controller Stephanie McConnell
Editorial Director Ruth O'Rourke
Art Director Maxine Pedliham
Publishing Director Stephanie Jackson

Editorial Clare Double
Design Studio Noel
Photography Jason Ingram

First published in Great Britain in 2026 by
Dorling Kindersley Limited
20 Vauxhall Bridge Road,
London SW1V 2SA

The authorised representative in the EEA is
Dorling Kindersley Verlag GmbH. Arnulfstr. 124,
80636 Munich, Germany

Text copyright © Simon Akeroyd 2026
Simon Akeroyd has asserted his right to be
identified as the author of this work.
Copyright © 2026 Dorling Kindersley Limited
A Penguin Random House Company
10 9 8 7 6 5 4 3 2 1
001–358273–Apr/2026

All rights reserved.
No part of this publication may be reproduced, stored in or introduced into a retrieval system, or transmitted, in any form, or by any means (electronic, mechanical, photocopying, recording, or otherwise), without the prior written permission of the copyright owner.

No part of this publication may be used or reproduced in any manner for the purpose of training artificial intelligence technologies or systems. In accordance with Article 4(3) of the DSM Directive 2019/790, DK expressly reserves this work from the text and data mining exception.

A CIP catalogue record for this book
is available from the British Library.
ISBN: 978-0-2418-0328-8

Printed and bound in China

www.dk.com

MIX
Paper | Supporting responsible forestry
FSC® C018179

This book was made with Forest Stewardship Council™ certified paper – one small step in DK's commitment to a sustainable future. Learn more at www.dk.com/uk/information/sustainability

About the author

Simon Akeroyd is the author of instant *Sunday Times* bestseller *Grow Your Groceries* and has written over 30 gardening books.

In 2022 he started a TikTok account dedicated to non-gardeners. His aim was to show just how easy – and fun – growing plants can be, and that it's always worth having a go. He's enjoyed huge engagement and has since expanded to Facebook and Instagram, where the audience has now overtaken his TikTok account. Simon now has over two million followers on social media.

Simon also runs one-day gardening experiences based on his books as Simon Akeroyd's Gardening Academy, which he hosts in Surrey and Devon.

He was previously Garden Manager for both the Royal Horticultural Society (RHS) and National Trust. Gardens he has managed include RHS Wisley, Polesden Lacey, RHS Harlow Carr, Sheffield Park, Coleton Fishacre, Agatha Christie's Greenway, and most recently Painshill in Surrey.

In his spare time Simon loves canoeing on the River Dart or exploring Dartmoor (and usually getting lost). He's currently writing a collection of Murder Mystery short stories with a horticultural twist.

Instagram: @simonakeroydgardenwriter
TikTok: @simonakeroydgardener
www.simonakeroyd.com